GUIDE FOR CELEBRATING

CHRISTIAN INITIATION

WITH ADULTS

VICTORIA M. TUFANO
PAUL TURNER
D. TODD WILLIAMSON

LITURGY
TRAINING
PUBLICATIONS

Nihil Obstat
Very Reverend Daniel A. Smilanic, JCD
Vicar for Canonical Services
Archdiocese of Chicago
August 1, 2016

Imprimatur
Very Reverend Ronald A. Hicks
Vicar General
Archdiocese of Chicago
August 1, 2016

The *Nihil Obstat* and *Imprimatur* are declarations that the material is free from doctrinal or moral error, and thus is granted permission to publish in accordance with c. 827. No legal responsibility is assumed by the grant of this permission. No implication is contained herein that those who have granted the *Nihil Obstat* and *Imprimatur* agree with the content, opinions, or statements expressed.

This book was edited by Mary Fox. Víctor R. Pérez was the production editor, Anna Manhart was the series designer, Juan A. Castillo was cover designer, and Kari Nicholls was the production artist.

Cover photo by Danielle A. Noe, MDIV. Photo on page 136 by Karen Callaway; photos on pages 18, 126, 131 by Andrew Kennedy Lewis © Liturgy Training Publications; photo on page 15 by Bishop Carl F. Mengeling; photo on pages 83, 89 © Antonio Pérez; photos on pages 4–6, 9, 17, 22–23, 31, 33–36, 38, 41, 49, 51, 56, 57, 59, 62–63, 67, 69, 70, 75, 79, 82, 84–85, 87, 88, 92, 95, 103–104, 111–112, 115–119, 121–122, 127, 130, 135 © John Zich.

Art on page vii © Martin Erspamer; on page 12 by Laura James © LTP.

This book is part of the *Preparing Parish Worship*™ series.

21 20 19 18 17   1 2 3 4 5

Printed in the United States of America.

Library of Congress Control Number: 2016954111

ISBN 978-1-61671-316-4

EGCCIA

CONTENTS

PREFACE

Apelles sat alone in his home finishing lunch when Andronicus and Junia barged into the room. They motioned with their hands for him to get up. They pointed out the window. Apelles wondered, "Where do they want me to go now?" He swallowed the last bit of bread and washed it down with a swig of wine. He shook his head and smiled, as if to say, "Here we go again." They were off.

Andronicus and Junia spoke to each other excitedly. Although he could not hear, Apelles could tell that something unusual was happening. He had hoped to take a nap after lunch. He could have objected to this spree. Even with his speech impediment he could communicate basic ideas to these close friends. But what was the point? He recognized their utter determination to get him out of the house and onto the road.

Around the bend a crowd had gathered to listen to a man speak. Apelles did not recognize the stranger and, of course, he could not hear anything the man said. But it was clear that everyone who had ears to hear listened intently. The man looked like a Galilean. His luminous face practically reflected the sun. His dark eyes saw into each person before him. The stranger moved his lips with such deliberate diction that when he turned toward Apelles, it was easy to discern each word: "Do you not realize that everything that goes into a person from outside cannot defile?"[1] Apelles was impressed with the obvious joy these words were bringing to the crowd, but he wondered, "What else is he saying? Why did my friends bring me to a lecture when they know I cannot hear?"

Finally the man looked directly at Apelles. Andronicus and Junia were speaking with him, pleading with him. They placed their hands on Apelles' head and motioned for the man to come do the same.[2] The man lifted the palm of one hand toward them as if telling them to wait. He spoke a while longer, apparently completing his argument. People looked at each other.

---

1. Mark 7:18.
2. Mark 7:32.

They nodded at the speaker. Finally the man ended his talk. But the crowd did not disperse.

He came up to Apelles and took his hand, leading him across the road behind a large rock, away from the crowd.[3] The man looked intently into the face of Apelles. He brushed his hands to loosen the dust from the road, and a small cloud enshrouded them both. The man extended both his index fingers and stretched his arms toward the sides of Apelles' head.

"Wait a minute," Apelles thought. He had clearly seen Andronicus and Junia placing their hands on top of his head as a signal for the man. "He's doing something else," he feared.

The man placed a finger inside each of Apelles' ears.[4] Although Apelles could not speak clearly, he could make sounds. He tried to say, "What do you think you're doing?" But the words came out—as usual—in indistinguishable vowels, completely lacking diction.

The man removed his fingers from Apelles' ears and drew his hands toward his own face, where he cupped them. Then he spat.[5] Several times. Apelles jerked his head back. He found the action strange, even revolting. But something else had alarmed him. He did not merely see the man spitting. He heard him hacking.

Apelles' mouth fell open in wonder. The man's hand was now dripping with spittle, which he disgustingly wiped inside Apelles' mouth directly onto his tongue.[6] Now Apelles wanted to spit, but he could not. The man's spittle tasted sweeter than honey.

The man looked up to heaven and groaned. Then he lowered his head and fixed his eyes on Apelles. "*Ephphatha!*" he shouted.[7]

Apelles could not contain his amazement any longer. "I heard that!" he exclaimed. He actually exclaimed. He exclaimed clearly.[8] Melodiously. With diction.

Andronicus and Junia came running around the rock, followed by the entire crowd of those who had been listening to the stranger.

"Apelles! Apelles! Can you hear me?" they each asked. He was stunned. "Yes. Yes. Oh. I can even hear my voice!"

---

3. Mark 7:33.
4. Mark 7:33.
5. Mark 7:33.
6. Mark 7:33.
7. Mark 7:34.
8. Mark 7:35.

Everyone started shouting. "Jesus has healed Apelles! Jesus has healed Apelles!" Apelles asked, "Who is Jesus?"

Jesus called out, "Friends, children—please, please. Others will not understand. Be silent. Don't talk. Keep your mouths shut. Do not say a word."[9]

"Do not say a word?" Apelles asked. "But you just gave me speech!"

Jesus took several steps back, turned, and then ran away from all of them. The others did not obey what he asked. In spite of his wishes they kept saying, "He has done all things well. He makes the deaf hear and the mute speak."[10]

Apelles opened his mouth. Then he closed it. He obeyed. And ran. He ran to follow Jesus.

Generations of Christians have related the account of Jesus curing the deaf man with the speech impediment. The story is so old that it kept the original Aramaic word that Jesus spoke on this occasion. The word *Ephphatha* appears even in the earliest Greek manuscripts of the Gospel according to Mark.

As early Christians drew new followers into a preparatory stage called the *catechumenate*, they took delight in this particular miracle. This process continues today. In the Gospel, the man could not hear at all and could not speak well, just as today many people have not yet heard about Christ and are unable to speak about him clearly. Friends who had discovered Jesus invited the man to meet him, just as today sponsors and members of the Christian community invite others to experience Christ through his word and their testimony. The companions of the man asked Jesus to place his hands on their friend, just as ministers today impose hands on catechumens at different stages of their formation. Jesus took the man apart from the crowd, just as those who enter a catechumenate today meet apart from the rest of the community to learn more about Christ. Jesus opened the man's ears and loosened his tongue, and today's minister of Baptism imitates the actions of this miracle in a ceremony called the

---

9. Mark 7:36.
10. Mark 7:37.

"Ephphetha"—the Aramaic word retained in the Gospel and still pronounced in the liturgy. As a result of this prayer, and as a result of Baptism, new Christians still proclaim the faith that they have heard, winning more disciples for Jesus Christ.

As Jesus prayed for the man to be opened, so the community prays that others may be opened to hear and proclaim the Gospel, especially through their participation in the *Rite of Christian Initiation of Adults*.

—Paul Turner

WELCOME

Christian initiation is the responsibility of all the baptized, the *Rite of Christian Initiation of Adults* tells us. It is a collaborative effort of every person in the parish. Those seeking to embrace the Christian faith in the Catholic Church learn how to follow Christ from his followers. Some will teach in formal ways, while others will teach by welcoming people into their lives and activities. Those who prepare and lead the many liturgies, great and small, will teach how to pray, how to find strength in God's blessing, and how to participate in liturgical prayer so that these inquirers and catechumens may eventually take their place at the celebration of the Eucharist on the day of their Baptism and for the rest of their lives.

The initiation rites are not the domain of a segment of the community. They belong to everyone. When celebrated well, they invite the community to embrace its newest members and to rejoice with them. When celebrated in a consistent manner over time, these rites become a welcome part of the community's repertoire of prayer.

Celebrated well, the rites during the initiation process help deepen the faith of the catechumens and of the faithful who participate in them. The faithful recall through the rites what it means to embrace the cross of Christ, to hear the Word of God deeply, to turn from sin and embrace the Gospel, and to profess faith in the Triune God who is always among us. They remember that, like the catechumens, they are on a journey of faith.

About This Book

The *Rite of Christian Initiation of Adults* is our era's guide to implementing the long and storied practice of Christian initiation, which arose from the charge the Lord Jesus gave his disciples: "Go, therefore, and make disciples of all nations, baptizing them in the name of the Father, and of the Son, and of the holy Spirit, teaching them to observe all that I have commanded you."[1]

---

1. Matthew 28:19–20.

Every age has responded to this charge in a way that reflects the culture and needs of the Church in that day. We are no different.

We live in a time when religious practice is no longer the norm for many people, and faith of any kind is often handed on to the next generation with only a perfunctory nod to tradition, as infants are baptized but later receive no religious formation. Many who were once practicing members of faith communities leave because they question Church teaching, no longer find that being part of the Church is enriching or convenient, or because they disagree with Church leaders or policies.

We also live in a time when people are hungry for meaning, for a way to live with truth and integrity. Jesus' charge to his disciples is as urgent today as it was when he first said it. This Church must seek to make disciples. We must constantly proclaim the Gospel of Jesus Christ in our words and in our lives.

> It is a task and mission which the vast and profound changes of present-day society make all the more urgent. Evangelizing is in fact the grace and vocation proper to the Church, her deepest identity. She exists in order to evangelize, that is to say, in order to preach and teach, to be the channel of the gift of grace, to reconcile sinners with God, and to perpetuate Christ's sacrifice in the Mass, which is the memorial of His death and glorious resurrection.[2]

Those who work in the ministry of Christian initiation know that people hear and see how we proclaim the Gospel. Many of them come to us seeking to hear more about what we believe, who we believe in, and why we do what we do, in church and outside church. Many others come to renew a faith long dormant or never fully formed. Others are active, faithful Christians who seek to live their faith in the Catholic communion. The *Rite of Christian Initiation of Adults* (RCIA) addresses all of these situations, but it is primarily concerned with unbaptized people coming to faith in Jesus Christ for the first time.

It would be helpful to the reader of this book to have a copy of the RCIA at hand. Please notice that the initials RCIA will be used in this book only to refer to the ritual text. The journey of those coming to faith will be called the initiation process, or the catechumenal process, or the catechumenal journey.

---

2. *Evangelii nuntiandi*, 14

This book focuses on the rites for the unbaptized adults. Because the book is addressed to those who prepare parish worship, it does not consider the Rite of Election, the Rite of Recognition of the Candidates by the Bishop and the Call to Continuing Conversion, and the rite combining the two.

What about the children? Liturgy Training Publications has also just published *Guide for Celebrating® Christian Initiation with Children*, by Rita Burns Senseman, Victoria M. Tufano, Paul Turner, and D. Todd Williamson.

About the Authors

VICTORIA M. TUFANO is senior editor and liturgical consultant at Liturgy Training Publications. She has served as a parish director of liturgy and Christian initiation and as a diocesan director of worship. She was a team member for institutes of the North American Forum on the Catechumenate and served on Forum's board of directors. She is a frequent writer and speaker on liturgy and Christian initiation, and was the editor of *Catechumenate: A Journal of Christian Initiation* and of several books on initiation. She holds a master of arts degree in liturgical studies and a master of divinity, both from the University of Notre Dame.

PAUL TURNER is pastor of St. Anthony Parish in Kansas City, Missouri. A priest of the Diocese of Kansas City-St. Joseph, he holds a doctorate in sacred theology from Sant'Anselmo in Rome. His publications include *At the Supper of the Lamb* (Chicago: Liturgy Training Publications, 2011); *Glory in the Cross* (Collegeville: Liturgical Press, 2011); *ML Bulletin Inserts* (Chicago: Liturgy Training Publications, 2012); and *Celebrating Initiation: A Guide for Priests* (Chicago: World Library Publications, 2008). He is a former president of the North American Academy of Liturgy, and a member of *Societas Liturgica* and the Catholic Academy of Liturgy. He is the 2013 recipient of the *Jubilate Deo* Award (National Association of Pastoral Musicians) and the Frederick McManus Award (Federation of Diocesan Liturgical Commissions). He serves as a facilitator for the International Commission on English in the Liturgy. Fr. Turner has provided the preface and the chapter "Theological and Historical Developments of Christian Initiation."

D. TODD WILLIAMSON is the director of the Office for Divine Worship in the Archdiocese of Chicago. He holds a master of arts in theological studies from Catholic Theological Union, in Chicago. He is the author of two editions of *Sourcebook for Sundays, Seasons, and Weekdays: The Almanac for*

Pastoral Liturgy (2007 and 2008) and has contributed to subsequent editions. He also has written for numerous periodicals, including *Rite, Pastoral Liturgy, Catechumenate: A Journal of Christian Initiation,* and *Religion Teacher's Journal.* He is the author, with Joe Paprocki, of *Great Is the Mystery: Encountering the Formational Power of Liturgy* (Chicago: Liturgy Training Publications, 2013). In addition to writing, Todd is a teacher and national speaker in the areas of liturgy and the sacraments.

SECTION 1

Preparing the Rites for Unbaptized Adults

The Theological and Historical Developments of Christian Initiation

As you sent me into the world, so I sent them into the world. And I consecrate myself for them, so that they also may be consecrated in truth.

—John 17:18–19

Christian Initiation, General Introduction

The meaning of Christian initiation in the Catholic Church is neatly summarized in the first paragraphs of *Christian Initiation*, General Introduction, which opens both the *Rite of Baptism for Children* and the *Rite of Christian Initiation of Adults* (RCIA).

At the time of the Second Vatican Council, when scholars reviewed the rituals then in force, they considered together the adult and the infant baptismal ceremonies. When they finished their work, they composed one "General Introduction" for initiation and attached both revised ceremonies to it in a single volume. However, in the end, the Vatican published the rites of Baptism for children and for adult initiation separately, each beginning with the same "General Introduction."

The first paragraph of the "General Introduction" details the three main purposes of Christian initiation, without ever mentioning the sacraments by name. These sacraments free us "from the power of darkness" and join us "to Christ's death, burial, and resurrection." They bestow "the Spirit of filial adoption," and they make us "part of the entire people of God in the celebration of the memorial of the Lord's death and resurrection."[1] Even without the subsequent paragraphs,

> In the sacraments of Christian initiation we are freed from the power of darkness and joined to Christ's death, burial, and resurrection.
>
> —*Christian Initiation*, General Introduction, 1

---

1. *Christian Initiation*, General Introduction (CI), 1.

these sentences clearly refer to Baptism, Confirmation, and the Eucharist. However, by omitting the names of the individual sacraments, the opening paragraph of the entire RCIA subtly proclaims that the initiation sacraments function as a unit. Even though each sacrament accomplishes something special, all work together to achieve something grand.

The second paragraph subdivides into sections that treat each initiation sacrament individually. "Baptism incorporates us into Christ and forms us into God's people."[2] This statement voices a positive view toward the purpose of Baptism.

The first paragraph of *Christian Initiation* states that the initiation sacraments act as a unit.

Prior to the Council, Catholics commonly learned a negative view: Baptism cleansed a person from Original Sin. It removed an obstacle to grace. The Church had embraced that definition largely because it supported the widespread pastoral practice of baptizing infants. The Church believes that Baptism cleanses a person from sin. The sins of an adult are easy to observe, but a child is incapable of personal sin. Nonetheless, the Church believes that every human being is born with Original Sin,[3] which the *Catechism of the Catholic Church* calls a sin "contracted," not "committed."[4] Original Sin characterizes the human condition that needs salvation. Baptism cleanses a human from this contracted sin, which explains one of the purposes of infant Baptism.

Although it is still correct to say that Baptism cleanses from Original Sin, the second paragraph of the "General Introduction" to *Christian Initiation* wants to stress two other points: incorporation into the Body of Christ and membership in God's people. Both concepts have strong biblical foundations. The letters of St. Paul call the community of the faithful "the body of Christ."[5] The First Letter of Peter calls the same community God's people.[6] The doctrine of Original Sin indicates what Baptism leaves behind, whereas the ideas of the Body of Christ and the People of God show where Baptism leads.

---

2. CI, 2.

3. Mary, because she was to become the mother of Jesus, was conceived without Original Sin, and therefore holds the title of the Immaculate Conception.

4. *Catechism of the Catholic Church*, (CCC), 404.

5. 1 Corinthians 12:27 and Romans 12:5.

6. 1 Peter 2:9–10.

The "General Introduction" makes other points about Baptism. It reaffirms that Baptism pardons all sins and rescues people from the power of darkness.[7] This relates to the foregoing point about Original Sin, but the introduction places these purposes of Baptism into a secondary field. It addresses the combat with sin and Satan only after proclaiming the victory of Jesus Christ.

> But you are a chosen race, a royal priesthood, a holy nation, a people of his own, "so that you may announce the praises of him who called you out of darkness into his wonderful light."
>
> —1 Peter 2:9

To conclude its initial reflection on Baptism, this paragraph introduces a mystical concept. The baptized are "a new creation," "adopted children," and "children of God."[8] The Church unflinchingly teaches that Jesus Christ is the Only Begotten Son of God. The New Testament affirms that those who follow him are also children of God,[9] and Jesus himself taught his followers to call upon God in prayer as their "Father." To distinguish Christ from Christians, the Church's tradition stresses that Jesus is the Only Begotten Son of God, but every Christian is an *adopted* child of God. St. Paul explores this analogy in two of his letters.[10] Baptism bestows an incomparable inheritance upon God's children.

With Confirmation, the Christian is signed, marked, and claimed as God's own.

The "General Introduction" next explores the Sacrament of Confirmation. Confirmation is a "signing . . . with the gift of the Spirit."[11] Although many Catholics assume that Confirmation is a personal acceptance of baptismal faith or an entrance into Christian adulthood, the official Church teachings never support this view. The Catechism explicitly warns that Confirmation should not be regarded as the "sacrament of Christian maturity."[12] Instead, one finds explanations consonant with the "General Introduction," which stresses that Confirmation

---

7. CI, 2.
8. CI, 2.
9. For example, 1 John 3:1.
10. Galatians 3:26 and Romans 8:14–17.
11. CI, 2.
12. CCC, 1308.

is a gift. It is a gift of the Holy Spirit, and with this gift, the Christian is signed, marked, and claimed as God's own.

Confirmation conveys some comparative properties. Not only does it draw one more closely to the Church, it makes the Christian "more completely the image of the Lord."[13] This presumes that a likeness to the image of the Lord has already taken effect at Baptism, and Confirmation polishes its results.

More significantly, the introduction states that Confirmation fills Christians with the Holy Spirit, "so that [they] may bear witness to him before all the world and work to bring the Body of Christ to its fullness as soon as possible."[14] These paired ideas are central to a proper understanding of Confirmation in the Catholic Church. It is a gift of the Holy Spirit, and that gift is given with a specific purpose in mind: the one who receives it is to bear witness to the faith before all the world. When Catholics baptized in infancy are preparing for Confirmation later in life, they commonly perform acts of Christian service to demonstrate their readiness for the sacrament. However, Confirmation has a more robust interest; it wants Christian service *after* the sacrament. It wants the newly confirmed to share the gifts of the Spirit broadly with a needy world.

The Eucharist is the sacramental participation in the Death and Resurrection of Jesus Christ.

A proper presentation on the Eucharist, of course, would require volumes, so the introduction shows admirable restraint by summarizing the purpose of this third initiation sacrament in just two sentences. The introduction affirms the central Catholic teaching about the Eucharist: the faithful "eat the flesh and drink the blood of the Son of Man." It states that Catholics do this "so that [they] may have eternal life and show forth the unity of God's people."[15] Thus, the Sacrament of the Eucharist pursues the initial goals of personal salvation and the unity of the People of God. But there is more.

---

13. CI, 2.
14. CI, 2.
15. CI, 2.

The Eucharist is not just about receiving and building. It is also about giving. The Eucharist is the sacramental participation in the Death and Resurrection of Jesus Christ, who offered himself for our salvation. Christians are expected to offer themselves with Christ, and to "share in the universal sacrifice."[16] This too has a purpose. The Church prays "for a greater outpouring of the Holy Spirit, so that the whole human race may be brought into the unity of God's family."[17] The Eucharist is such an awesome gift to humanity that it lures the faithful to meditate on their personal spiritual enrichment, rather than their personal spiritual calling. Yet that calling

> Those who have received the Good News and who have been gathered by it into the community of salvation can and must communicate and spread it.
>
> —*Evangelii nuntiandi*, 13

is real. Those who share in Communion, from their very first Communion, have evangelical responsibilities. They are to go and announce the Gospel of the Lord so that others may discover salvation in Christ.

In summary, the Introduction sees the close connection among the three sacraments of Christian initiation. It concludes by affirming their double purpose: these sacraments bring the faithful to the full stature of Christ, and they enable the faithful "to carry out the mission of the entire people of God in the Church and in the world."[18] These goals are immensely challenging, but they come with all the equipment that the faithful need—the grace that flows from the sacraments of Christian initiation.

The Periods of the Rite of Christian Initiation of Adults

The *Rite of Christian Initiation of Adults* brings unbaptized candidates through four stages and three transitional rites. The Period of Evangelization and Precatechumenate leads to the Rite of Acceptance into the Order of Catechumens. The Period of the Catechumenate leads to the Rite of Election or the Enrollment of Names. The Period of Purification and Enlightenment leads to the sacraments of initiation. The Period of Mystagogy extends beyond initiation. A good understanding of the entire *Rite of Christian Initiation of Adults* requires familiarity with the goals of these periods.

---

16. CI, 2.
17. CI, 2.
18. CI, 2.

Period of Evangelization and Precatechumenate

The Period of Evangelization presumes that those who have never been baptized may have had little experience of the Christian spiritual life. Consequently, during this period, "faithfully and constantly the living God is proclaimed and Jesus Christ whom he has sent for the salvation of all."[19] In fact, some of those who have never been baptized already have an experience of the living God and consider themselves followers of Jesus Christ. But the Period of Evangelization should not overlook some fundamental questions. This period explores the very basics of the spiritual life: "Who is God for this inquirer? What has he or she learned about Jesus Christ? Do these unbaptized inquirers consider themselves Christians already? Why?" And if they have little experience of Christ and the Gospel, the Period of Evangelization will fill this vacuum.

> For the Church, evangelizing means bringing the Good News into all the strata of humanity, and through its influence, transforming humanity and making it new.
> —*Evangelii nuntiandi*, 18

Period of the Catechumenate

The Period of the Catechumenate unveils more extensive catechesis. Whereas the previous period focused on basics, this period deepens the particulars. The pivotal paragraph is 75, which outlines four means by which catechesis is to be accomplished. This paragraph challenges parish leaders to employ various techniques of formation. Catechesis is not simply a matter of teaching "dogmas and precepts" through a plan that is "gradual and complete in its coverage," but also of helping the catechumens gain "a profound sense of the mystery of salvation" that these teachings represent.[20]

Many faithful catechists accept the wisdom of that broad description. The catechumenate is not a course in religious studies. It is an invitation to discipleship. However, some catechists may be surprised to learn that even this broader description of catechesis summarizes only the first of the four methods that RCIA, 75, espouses. The others include becoming familiar with "the Christian way of life," joining in "suitable liturgical rites," and learning "to spread the Gospel and build up the Church by the witness of their [the

---

19. RCIA, 36.
20. RCIA, 75 §1.

catechumens'] lives and by professing their faith."[21] The arc of catechesis extends beyond the classroom. It penetrates family life, where catechumens learn to imitate how Christians live. It includes the church building, where they follow the basic principles of worship. It may even touch workplaces or recreation areas, where the catechumens may bear witness to their faith before others. Even catechumens who lack the skills of basic literacy may accomplish the goals of RCIA, 75, where people learn about the Church not just from books, but from Christians, their liturgy, and their witness. All four of these factors contribute to the lively and essential formation of those who have decided to follow Christ.

During the Period of the Catechumenate, the catechumen not only comes to know the teachings of the Church, but also gains a sense of the mystery of salvation.

Period of Purification and Enlightenment

The third period of formation, which usually coincides with Lent, is called Purification and Enlightenment. Both concepts are important. During this time the prayers of the Church purify the elect from whatever is keeping them from following Christ, and enlighten and strengthen all the good that is drawing them forward toward the waters of Baptism.

The journey begins with the Rite of Election or Enrollment of Names. At this time the Church declares that those who have begun their formation are to be numbered among the "elect"; that is, among the new "chosen people" of God. Just as God chose Abraham and his descendants for a covenant, so God chooses people today for the covenant of Baptism. As Moses led his followers through the Red Sea into the Promised Land, so Christ leads his followers through discipleship to the waters of Baptism and the promised land of eternal life.

Along the way, the Period of Purification and Enlightenment deals intensely with the spiritual struggles that any of the elect may face. As Christ

---

21. RCIA, 75 §§2, 3, and 4.

battled Satan in the desert, a story recounted every year in the Gospel at Mass on the First Sunday of Lent, so the elect face the spiritual battle that will help them leave temptation behind and pursue the good. They will achieve victory through the help of the Holy Spirit. The Scrutinies that punctuate the Lenten season intend to bring the elect purification and enlightenment. Scrutinies exorcise the spirit of evil, and they infuse the Holy Spirit. Then, just before Baptism, the elect renounce Satan and profess faith in Christ Jesus, bringing these weeks of struggle to a

> The scrutinies are meant to uncover, then heal all that is weak, defective, or sinful in the hearts of the elect; to bring out, then strengthen all that is upright, strong, and good.
>
> —*Rite of Christian Initiation of Adults*, 141

head. They demonstrate that the Scrutinies have taken effect. They are turning away from sin and Satan, and turning toward Christ and the promise of eternal life. The whole Period of Purification and Enlightenment therefore consists "more in interior reflection than in catechetical instruction." It is a time of intense spiritual preparation.[22]

Period of Mystagogy

Mystagogy, the fourth and final period of formation, follows the initiation rites. The neophytes take their place with the entire community of the baptized, and all continue their experience of the sacraments. They meditate on the Gospel, share in the Eucharist, and perform works of charity.[23] The main setting for this mystagogy is the Sunday Masses of the Easter season.[24] There, through proclamation of the Gospel, preaching, and the celebration of the Eucharist, the newly baptized are formed for life as followers of Christ.

History of Christian Initiation

The Apostolic Church

Jesus commanded his followers to go out, teach, and baptize. Matthew's account of the Gospel concludes with this command,[25] and the apostolic Church immediately put it into practice. The Acts of the Apostles offers wide-

---

22. RCIA, 139.
23. RCIA, 244.
24. RCIA, 247.
25. Matthew 28:19–20.

spread testimony of early Baptisms, but a few examples will suffice. On Pentecost Day, having received the gifts of the Spirit, Peter preached about Christ to the assembled crowds, and about three thousand were baptized.[26] Philip successfully preached and baptized men and women who formerly adhered to Simon the magician.[27] Simon himself accepted Baptism.[28] Philip explained the prophecies of Isaiah to an Ethiopian eunuch, who requested and received Baptism in a nearby pool.[29] Peter preached to the members of the household of Cornelius and baptized them after they manifested gifts of the Holy Spirit.[30]

In these and other circumstances, the reader is struck by the immediate impact of the Gospel. Great numbers of people listened attentively to its message and believed. Conversion led to Baptism.

> Or are you unaware that we who were baptized into Christ Jesus were baptized into his death?
>
> —Romans 6:3

The New Testament lacks detailed information about the methods of Baptism. The word comes from the Greek verb for *to dip* or *to immerse*, so the very term implies dipping someone into water. Some passages suggest that Baptism required a large amount of water. Paul's letters twice compare Baptism to burial.[31] The First Letter of Peter likens Baptism to the flood of Noah.[32] Jesus appears to compare Baptism with birth when he calls followers to be born of water and the Spirit.[33] These passages support the idea that the first Baptisms brought believers completely underwater and up again as a sign of new life.

The Sacrament of Confirmation has its origins at Pentecost.[34] The Apostles witnessed those same gifts of the Holy Spirit falling upon other believers as well, notably at the household of Cornelius.[35] As a rule, the Apostles expected that gifts of the Holy Spirit would accompany Baptism, and were surprised when they did not.[36] Paul laid hands on a small group so

---

26. Acts 2:1–41.
27. Acts 8:12.
28. Acts 8:13.
29. Acts 8:26–39.
30. Acts 10:44–48.
31. Romans 6:3–4; Colossians 2:12.
32. 1 Peter 3:20–21.
33. John 3:5.
34. Acts 2:1–11.
35. Acts 10:44–46.
36. Acts 8:15–17; 19:6.

that they might receive the Holy Spirit.[37] His Second Letter to the Corinthians associates the gifts of the Spirit with anointing and sealing.[38] The First Letter of John also mentions that the first Christians were anointed.[39] The Letter to the Hebrews associates Baptism with the imposition of hands.[40] The New Testament lacks hard evidence that anointing and hand-laying customarily accompanied Baptism for the conferral of the Holy Spirit, but its language opened the door for the later development of actions associated with Confirmation.

At Pentecost, the Apostles witnessed the gifts of the Holy Spirit falling upon believers.

The baptized shared the Eucharist. Acts reports several times that the apostolic community broke bread,[41] a reference to the Eucharist. Paul wrote about the early Christian practice of sharing one cup and one loaf.[42] He gives the earliest testimony to the Eucharistic words of Jesus at the Last Supper.[43] Inspired by Jesus' command to "do this" in his memory, early Christians shared the Eucharist as a sign of their faithful discipleship.

The biblical roots of the initiation sacraments show the centrality of baptizing, receiving the gifts of the Holy Spirit, and sharing Communion. This ultimately shaped ritual practice.

The Patristic Era

As the Christian community settled into diverse regions, local initiation practices developed. Evidence shows some disparity in the procedures, yet uniformity in the most important elements such as Baptism and the Eucharist.

The late first-century *Didache*, a kind of early Christian handbook, described Baptism in running water in the name of the Trinity. It also restricted participation in the Eucharist to those who had been baptized.[44]

---

37. Acts 19:5–7.

38. 2 Corinthians 1:21–22.

39. 1 John 2:20, 27.

40. Hebrews 6:1–2.

41. Acts 2:42–47; 20:7–12; 27:33–38.

42. 1 Corinthians 10:16–17.

43. 1 Corinthians 11:23–25.

44. Paul Turner, *The Hallelujah Highway: A History of the Catechumenate* (Chicago: Liturgy Training Publications, 2000), p. 15.

Justin Martyr (†165) gave the earliest clear testimony of Baptisms taking place in the context of a Eucharist.[45] Clement of Alexandria (†215) recorded the earliest known usage of the word *catechumen*.[46] In North Africa, Tertullian (†220) offered more expansive evidence for the preparation and celebration of Baptism, an event he preferred to celebrate on Easter and Pentecost.[47] From Egypt, Origen (†253) told about anointing the baptized with oil.[48] These early witnesses showed the widespread interest in developing initiation rites.

Perhaps the most influential of the early sources is the one called the *Apostolic Tradition*, whose origins are much debated. For many years it was considered to be the work of St. Hippolytus, dating to the early third century and describing initiation rites in Rome. However, scholarship now proposes a slightly later date, extending even into the fourth century, and a broader range of potential geographical sources.[49] Its author and title are unknown, but it has to be called something, so the traditional title, the *Apostolic Tradition*, remains.

Its catechetical formation included Scripture, prayer, and handlaying, but the catechumens were expected to have contact with the community and to perform a variety of good works. Prior to Baptism they were examined again and underwent exorcisms and anointing. Professing faith in the Trinity, they were baptized three times in water. They were anointed again by the bishop, received hand-laying from him, and joined in Communion with bread, water, a mixture of milk and honey, and wine.[50] (The *Apostolic Tradition* was extremely influential in the development of the *Rite of Christian Initiation of Adults* after the Second Vatican Council.)

Contemporaneous to it was the *Apostolic Constitutions* from Syria. This work manifests a similar interest in preparing candidates for Baptism through catechetical formation and behavioral scrutiny. It also offers a healthy description of the initiation rites, including developed roles for deacons and deaconesses.[51]

Examples of mystagogical preaching tell more about the initiation ceremonies of this period. Cyril of Jerusalem (†387) was bishop at the time that

---

45. Turner, *Hallelujah Highway*, p. 18–20.

46. Turner, *Hallelujah Highway*, p. 23.

47. Turner, *Hallelujah Highway*, p. 28–30.

48. Turner, *Hallelujah Highway*, p. 34.

49. Paul Bradshaw, Maxwell E. Johnson, and L. Edward Phillips, *The Apostolic Tradition*, Hermeneia: A Critical and Historical Commentary on the Bible (Minneapolis: Fortress Press, 2002).

50. Turner, *Hallelujah Highway*, pp. 42–43.

51. Turner, *Hallelujah Highway*, pp. 47–48.

Egeria wrote her diary, which included a fascinating description of Holy Week services in the holy city.[52] Ambrose (†397) recounted the initiation practices in Milan, which included foot-washing as part of the baptismal liturgy. John Chrysostom (†407), once patriarch of Constantinople, preached eloquent homilies to the newly baptized, explaining many of the rites they experienced. He also used a baptismal formula in the passive voice: "N. is baptized in the name of the Father and of the Son and of the Holy Spirit."[53] Theodore of Mopsuestia (†428) also detailed the stages of catechumenal formation and initiation, adopting a process of moral and intellectual formation, as well as a series of rites from the submission of names to Baptism, anointing, and the Eucharist.[54] Augustine (†430) mentioned aspects of initiation ceremonies throughout many of his writings, including the use of salt for those becoming catechumens, the submission of names to the bishop, Scrutinies, the presentation of a creed that the catechumens were later to recite from memory, and the presentation of the Lord's Prayer. The initiation rites included Baptism, anointing, clothing, and participation in the Eucharist. The newly baptized wore their special garments to the Eucharist throughout the week of Easter.[55]

Sacramentaries and Pontificals

By the Middle Ages, Christianity had taken strong root throughout Europe. Most of the adults had been baptized, so clergy more commonly baptized infants. Still, evidence for the initiation rites can be found in the sacramentaries and pontificals developed during this time. Most of these detail the ministry of bishops because they sought books to execute the ceremonies correctly and because they had access to the laborers and financial resources required to produce the books.

The seventh-century *Gelasian Sacramentary* included liturgical prayers for events such as making an unbaptized adult a catechumen. It included prayers for Scrutiny Masses, as well as for the presentations of the Gospels, the Creed, and the Lord's Prayer. It recommended Baptism at Easter. The newly baptized were anointed, and they shared in the Eucharist.[56] (Some of these prayers have been preserved in the post-Vatican II Missal.)

---

52. Turner, *Hallelujah Highway*, pp. 54–55.
53. Turner, *Hallelujah Highway*, p. 70.
54. Turner, *Hallelujah Highway*, pp. 75–76.
55. Turner, *Hallelujah Highway*, pp. 65–66.
56. Turner, *Hallelujah Highway*, pp. 95–99.

By the tenth century the rites of initiation reappeared in the *Roman-Germanic Pontifical*, which contained two procedures: the now traditional suite of ceremonies extending through Lent and culminating at Easter and Pentecost, and a condensed version in which the various rites were combined into a single ceremony. This latter ceremony presumably developed for the Baptism of infants.[57] In the *Roman Pontifical* of the twelfth century, only a version of this second option appears. All the preliminary rites of Lent had been omitted. The catechumenal and baptismal ceremonies all took place on one day.[58]

Several decades after the Council of Trent, the Vatican combined and updated its non-Eucharistic ceremonies in the 1614 *Roman Ritual*. The order of Baptism appears twice—an extended ritual for adults and an abbreviated version for infants.

A subcommittee of the consilium that Pope Paul VI authorized during the Second Vatican Council revised the *Rite of Baptism for Children* and the *Rite of Christian Initiation of Adults*.

The various ceremonies of the catechumenate were combined into a single event, though without Confirmation and the Eucharist.[59] This book remained in force for more than three hundred fifty years.

Meanwhile, missionary movements were appealing to the Vatican for a catechumenate in stages. As evangelization spread to new areas remote from long-established Christian churches, missionaries in Africa, Latin America, and Asia saw an advantage to offering ceremonies in stages. The Sacred Congregation for the Propagation of the Faith encouraged the development of catechesis, though it hesitated to embrace dividing up the baptismal liturgy as it then appeared in the Roman Ritual.[60] Still, the experience of missionaries was demonstrating that dividing the ceremony back into its parts had catechetical, spiritual, and liturgical merit. On the eve of the Second Vatican Council in 1962, the Vatican approved a catechumenate in stages,[61]

57. Turner, *Hallelujah Highway*, p. 106.
58. Turner, *Hallelujah Highway*, p. 109.
59. Turner, *Hallelujah Highway*, p. 138.
60. Turner, *Hallelujah Highway*, p. 140.
61. Turner, *Hallelujah Highway*, p. 155.

but the catechumenate enjoyed comparatively minor usage until the Council's liturgical renewal set forth a new design.

The Consilium

While the Second Vatican Council was still in session, Pope Paul VI authorized a special consilium for the implementation of the *Constitution on the Sacred Liturgy*. One of the subcommittess of the consilium took on the task of revising the *Rite of Baptism for Children* and the *Rite of Christian Initiation of Adults*. The committee began its work with the order of adult initiation, which gave them the background against which to apply its principles of initiation to the order of Baptism for children.

Committee members each had expertise in some pertinent area: canon law, sacraments, academics, pastoral ministry, missionary outreach, and history, for example. The group studied in particular the *Apostolic Tradition*, and its historical relationship to the growing Church of the patristic era. By 1966 the committee had completed a draft of the order of adult initiation, which was sent to fifty pastoral centers around the world for comment. Feedback poured in from Japan, Indonesia, Mali, Togo, the Ivory Coast, Upper Volta, Rwanda, Zaire, Congo, Belgium, France, Canada, and the United States.[62]

The Vatican published the revised rite in 1972. A provisional English translation became available in 1974, and the official English translation was approved in 1988. This final book included the rites of Christian initiation for the unbaptized, and sections pertaining to special circumstances such as unbaptized children of catechetical age, those with a need for initiation apart from the Easter Vigil, unbaptized persons in danger of death, persons baptized Catholic as infants but lacking further catechetical formation and participation in the sacraments, and even persons baptized validly in other Christian communities now seeking admission to the full communion of the Roman Catholic Church. The extensive work of the Consilium bore fruit in unexpected ways. Although the rite

> The catechumenate for adults, divided into several stages, is to be restored and put into use at the discretion of the local Ordinary. By this means the time of the catechumenate . . . may be sanctified by sacred rites to be celebrated at successive intervals of time.
>
> —*Constitution on the Sacred Liturgy*, 64

---

62. Turner, *Hallelujah Highway*, p. 157.

The *Rite of Christian Initiation of Adults* is among the most far-reaching exponents of the Second Vatican Council.

developed at the request of missionaries in Africa and Asia, it established a firm foothold in places where Christianity had been in place for many centuries. The formulas for discerning discipleship applied evenly to people of many cultures and climes. Outside Roman Catholicism, other Christian communities took notice and prepared ceremonies paralleling the work that the Consilium completed.

The Second Vatican Council made a tremendous impact on the life of the Catholic Church. One of its most far-reaching exponents was the *Rite of Christian Initiation of Adults.*

An Introduction to the *Rite of Christian Initiation of Adults*

When the holy Spirit, who calls all women and men to Christ and arouses
in their hearts the submission of faith by the seed of the word and
the preaching of the gospel, brings those who believe in Christ to a new
life through the womb of the baptismal font, he gathers them into one
people of God which is a "chosen race, a royal priesthood, a holy
nation, a purchased people" (1 Pet 2:9).

—*Ad gentes*, 15

The *Rite of Christian Initiation of Adults* (RCIA) is an official rite of the Roman Catholic Church, part of the collection of rites that together comprise the Roman Ritual. The other rites included in the Roman Ritual are those that every priest needs, such as the *Rite of Baptism for Children*, the *Rite of Penance*, and the *Order of Celebrating Matrimony*.

The directives in the *Rite of Christian Initiation of Adults* describe how to bring a person to faith in Jesus Christ and membership in the Church.

This may be more than anyone needs to know before implementing the RCIA, but it is important to understand that this rite carries the same weight in the Church as the other sacramental rites. The catechetical, liturgical, and pastoral directives it contains describe the Church's understanding of how best to bring an adult or a child old enough to understand to faith in Jesus Christ and membership in his Body, the Church.

The book in which the *Rite of Christian Initiation of Adults* is published contains the document itself as well as a few others. It is helpful to become familiar with what the book contains and especially how the rite itself is organized.

Official Statements

Even before the table of contents, the decree stating that this rite is published with all the necessary approvals is found. It also notes that the use of this rite is mandatory, beginning September 1, 1988. This decree is from the National Conference of Catholic Bishops, which is now called the United States Conference of Catholic Bishops. A similar decree is found in the Canadian edition.

In the foreword, the Bishops' Committee on the Liturgy, now called the Bishops' Committee on Divine Worship, offers helpful information on how to understand the book's contents.

Finally, the 1972 decree declared the Latin text as the *editio typica* for the Christian initiation of adults, replacing the previous rites. The *editio typica* is the basis for the translations of the rite into other languages.

Christian Initiation, General Introduction

When the *Rite of Baptism for Children* (RBC) was published in Latin in 1969, it included an introduction to the rite itself, as all rites do; such introductions are also called *praenotanda*. In addition, the (RBC) included a general introduction to Christian initiation, which set the Baptism of children into a larger understanding of Christian initiation that included the three sacraments of initiation. The committee of scholars that produced the renewed *Rite of Baptism for Children* was also responsible for shaping the *Rite of Christian Initiation of Adults,* which would be published three years later; this general introduction was written to be appropriate for both rites.

Christian Initiation, General Introduction, provides a solid basis for understanding the importance of Baptism and the dignity of the baptized. It also provides information regarding the role of godparents and the regulations concerning them, the administration of Baptism in an emergency situation, and the place for Baptism.

The Rite of Christian Initiation of Adults

Finally, the document itself. The rite is divided into two main sections.

Part I, titled "Christian Initiation of Adults," deals with the evangelization and formation of unbaptized, uncatechized adults and the rites that are appropriate to them as they make the journey from inquiring about the

Christian faith and the Catholic Church to full initiation through the Sacraments of Baptism, Confirmation, and Eucharist and beyond.

Part II, titled "Rites for Particular Circumstances," builds on Part I. It offers adaptations that are appropriate to people in situations similar to unbaptized, uncatechized adults, but different enough to warrant significant changes in how the Church ministers to them. These include unbaptized children who have reached catechetical age (who are considered to be adults under Church law for most situations but whose religious and developmental needs are different from those who have reached the age of majority); adults in exceptional circumstances or in danger of death; and baptized adult Christians. This last group includes people baptized in the Catholic Church who were never catechized and so were neither confirmed nor received the Eucharist. It also includes those baptized in other Christian communions who were not catechized and who wish to be received into the full communion of the Catholic Church. Part II also contains the rite for the Reception of Baptized Christians into the Full Communion of the Catholic Church.

Appendices

Three appendices are found in the back of the book.

Appendix I contains combined rites for times when catechumens and baptized candidates for reception into the full communion of the Catholic Church celebrate similar times of transition. These rites are adaptations made for the United States.

Appendix II presents Scripture acclamations, hymns in the style of the New Testament, and songs from ancient liturgies. These could be useful as chants or acclamations during catechumenal rites, or as texts for reflection.

Appendix III contains the *National Statutes for the Catechumenate*, which are particular law for the United States regarding how Christian initiation is to be carried out. These statutes were passed by the bishops of the United States and confirmed by the Holy See. It is important that those who minister in Christian initiation are familiar with these statutes.

Baptism by immersion is the fuller and more expressive sign of the sacrament and, therefore, provision should be made for its more frequent use in the baptism of adults.

—*National Statutes for the Catechumenate*, 17

Preparing the Rite of Acceptance into the Order of Catechumens

Although the rite of initiation begins with admission to the catechumenate, the preceding period or precatechumenate is of great importance and as a rule should not be omitted. It is a time of evangelization: faithfully and constantly the living God is proclaimed and Jesus Christ whom he has sent for the salvation of all. Thus those who are not yet Christians, their hearts opened by the Holy Spirit, may believe and be freely converted to the Lord and commit themselves sincerely to him.

—*Rite of Christian Initiation of Adults*, 36

The Period of Evangelization and Precatechumenate

The initiation process formally begins with the celebration of the Rite of Acceptance into the Order of Catechumens, but the Period of Evangelization and Precatechumenate that precedes it is crucial. During this time, which may begin long before an individual approaches the Christian community, God touches the heart and draws the person to seek to know him through Jesus Christ.

This may occur in many ways. A person may be touched by a Christian friend or acquaintance's generosity, kindness, or hope during a time of trial. Or an individual may respond to an article or interview on some aspect of Christian teaching. Perhaps these seekers are moved by the Church's care for the poor, call for justice, or witness to the sanctity of life. They may have been moved by a word of peace or mercy from a preacher. They may be seeking a deeper meaning to life or experiencing a desire to live in a different manner. Many times, they fall in love with a person of faith. However it happens, being drawn to the Church is a sign of God at work in people's lives, inviting them to know and love him.

The Christian community is charged during the Period of Evangelization and Precatechumenate with evangelizing the person who has responded to God's invitation. This person often is referred to as an *inquirer*.

Faithfully and constantly the living God is proclaimed and Jesus Christ whom he has sent for the salvation of all. Thus those who are not yet

Christians, their hearts opened by the Holy Spirit, may believe and be freely converted to the Lord and commit themselves sincerely to him. For he who is the way, the truth, and the life fulfills all their spiritual expectations, indeed infinitely surpasses them.[1]

The purpose of evangelization is to make known the living God, especially as he is revealed through Jesus Christ. Two primary ways people come to know Christ are the Scriptures and the Church.

During the Period of the Precatechumenate, the Old and New Testaments must be shared in a way that salvation as a historic and continuing work of God is revealed. As we do this, we cannot presume that people are familiar with Scripture. Many of the inquirers will have heard Bible stories as children or seen film versions, but some will have seemingly little biblical knowledge. It is important that the inquirers become acquainted with Scripture as the basis of our faith.

People come to know God through the sharing of Scripture.

People also come to know Christ through the Church. During this period, it is especially important that the inquirers come to know Christ through those who know him through faith. These include the saints to whom we look for inspiration and the living members of our Church communities experiencing the joys and struggles of the life of faith now. Their relationships with Christ and their stories of faith are another important way that inquirers come to know the Lord.

Inquirers usually have many questions about the Church; hearing and understanding the answers help them build their relationship with the Church. Questions may be simple or challenging. If the answer to a query isn't readily known, the individual questioned should admit the lack of knowledge and say they will get back with the answer after doing research. Inquirers may ask the meaning of a particular symbol or image, or they may want to discuss something they have heard about the Church in the news. They may wonder why Catholics do a particular thing or why a good God allows bad things to happen. Their questions may also be more personal, requiring individual conversation with a priest, another trained minister, or a counselor.

---

1. RCIA, 36.

An element of Catholic teaching that needs to be approached with the inquirer is the permanency of marriage. Early in the precatechumenate, even as early as the initial interview, the inquirer should be asked privately whether he or she has been divorced and remarried, and whether the inquirer's spouse has been. If this is the case with either party, it will be necessary to discuss the Church's annulment process. This is best done by a person knowledgeable about the process and the reasons for it; the pastor or another minister who works with annulments will need to help with the necessary paperwork.

Not everyone will want to participate in the annulment process. The decision of whether to do so will be part of the inquirer's discernment about the initiation journey. If choosing to seek an annulment, the individual needs to know that the length of time for completing the process cannot be guaranteed, and that the sacraments of initiation (and, usually, the Rite of Election) cannot be celebrated until the annulment is granted. A person who has been divorced and has not remarried may continue toward the initiation sacraments but will need an annulment to remarry.

Inquirers should be made to feel welcome at parish events.

Relations with the Church are also built as individuals socialize with the Christian community. Inquirers should know they are welcome to attend parish-wide events. There, they might be introduced to parishioners who are at similar stages in life—early adulthood, recently or soon-to-be married, parents, singles, retirees—or to people with similar interests, such as book group members and movie buffs. People just coming to the Church may be testing whether there is a way for them to fit into parish life. Bonds of friendship and shared interests often help sustain faith.

Like all relationships, the relationship with God in Christ is strengthened and deepened through communication. Inquirers should be encouraged to begin to pray if they have not already done so. Discussing the reasons for prayer—blessing and adoration, petition, intercession, and thanksgiving—and the customary times for prayer may help the inquirers understand how prayer fits into their lives. Different types of personal prayer could be introduced to help the inquirer begin the practice of regular prayer.

There are no formal prayers or rituals prescribed for this period, but clergy, catechists, and sponsors should begin and end their time with the inquirers with prayer. Blessings and prayers of exorcism provided in the rite for the Period of the Catechumenate[2] may be appropriate.[3]

The aim of evangelization is to help inquirers to come to know Christ so that they can enter a relationship with him and be converted to him. Conversion is the heart of the Christian initiation process. The Period of Evangelization and the Precatechumenate must be conducted in such a way that the inquirer's relationship with God,

> From evangelization, completed with the help of God, come the faith and initial conversion that cause a person to feel called away from sin and drawn into the mystery of God's love.
>
> —*Rite of Christian Initiation of Adults*, 37

which began at God's initiative, is fostered and deepened. "During this period, priests and deacons, catechists and other laypersons are to give the candidates a suitable explanation of the Gospel. The candidates are to receive help and attention so that with a purified and clearer intention they may cooperate with God's grace."[4]

This cooperation with God's grace is manifested in many ways, including a desire to live in accord with God's Word and to repent of those times in their lives that they have not done so. During this period, it is important that inquirers build a relationship of trust with clergy, sponsors, and other members of the community with whom they can discuss these changes in their lives.

The Period of Evangelization and Precatechumenate is very flexible. The period does not correspond with a particular time of the liturgical or calendar year, and there is no set length or end date. This is really a season of an individual's life during which they begin to respond in a formal way to God's invitation to enter into a relationship of faith. It is our responsibility to support and foster that developing faith.

---

2. RCIA, 94, 97.
3. RCIA, 40.
4. RCIA, 38.

Discernment Prior to the Rite of Acceptance

The Period of Evangelization and Precatechumenate ends with the celebration of the Rite of Acceptance into the Order of Catechumens. Before this rite is celebrated, the inquirer and the Church, represented by the clergy, catechists, sponsors, and others, discern whether this is the right time for the inquirer to move to the next period.[5] The guidelines the rite offers for discerning the inquirer's readiness also provide an overview of what should occur during the precatechumenate.

> The prerequisite for making this first step is that the beginnings of the spiritual life and the fundamentals of Christian teaching have taken root in the candidates. Thus there must be evidence of the first faith that was conceived during the period of evangelization and precatechumenate and of an initial conversion and intention to change their lives and to enter into a relationship with God in Christ. Consequently, there must also be evidence of the first stirrings of repentance, a start to the practice of calling upon God in prayer, a sense of the Church, and some experience of the company and spirit of Christians through contact with a priest or with members of the community. The candidates should also be instructed about the celebration of the liturgical rite of acceptance.[6]

The whole period of the precatechumenate is set aside for this evangelization, so that the genuine will to follow Christ and seek baptism may mature.
—*Rite of Christian Initiation of Adults*, 37

During the Rite of Acceptance into the Order of Catechumens, inquirers declare to the Christian community their intention to become members of the Church, and the Church accepts them as such.

This ritual changes the status of the person undergoing it from an outsider to an insider, from a guest to a member of the household, from an inquirer to a catechumen. "From this time on the Church embraces the catechumens as its own with a mother's love and concern."[7] One who is a catechumen has a recognized status in the Church. He or she is "part of the household of Christ,"[8]

---

5. RCIA, 43.
6. RCIA, 42.
7. RCIA, 47.
8. RCIA, 47.

although not yet a full member. Catechumens may be married in the Church with the appropriate rite, and they may receive a Christian burial.[9]

Preparing for the Rite of Acceptance into the Order of Catechumens

The Rite of Acceptance should be prepared so that it is an integral part of the liturgy and should be celebrated with the same care and preparation that characterize the rest of the parish's liturgical life. The director of the catechumenal process should work with the celebrant, the liturgy director, and the music director to prepare this liturgy. It may be helpful to begin preparing this and the other rites that are part of the initiation process long before the Rite of Acceptance is scheduled. Such preparation will lend cohesion to the way the rites are celebrated in a given year and over a longer period of time.

> The prerequisite for making this first step is that the beginnings of the spiritual life and the fundamentals of Christian teaching have taken root in the candidates.
>
> —*Rite of Christian Initiation of Adults,* 42

Those who prepare the Rite of Acceptance into the Order of Catechumens must understand how it is different from most of the sacramental celebrations and blessings that occur at Mass. Most rites takes place after the Word of God is proclaimed and preached. The Rite of Acceptance, however, is literally an entrance rite, during which the inquirers ask to be admitted into the household of faith and the assembled Church welcomes them. This rite replaces the usual Introductory Rites of the Mass, just as does the Reception of the Children when infant Baptism is celebrated at Mass. The Penitential Act and the Gloria are omitted when the Rite of Acceptance occurs.

To symbolize that the inquirers are moving from outside the Church to inside, the rite ideally begins outside the church. The preparers of the liturgy must consider the space in the interior and exterior of the building when determining where the rite will take place. At least a representative portion of the assembly should be able to be accommodated in the space. A plaza in front of the church, a large narthex or gathering space, a hall, or other large room would be appropriate. If no such space is available, it may take place just inside the church doors.[10] Wherever the rite begins, preparers must

---

9. RCIA, 47.
10. RCIA, 48.

consider how the assembly will participate. They should be able to see, to hear, and to respond in word and song.

The signing of the inquirers on the forehead and, often, on all the senses, is an important aspect of this rite. In the preparation of this rite, it is important to be aware that the signing is done by touching the forehead and other parts of the body. This should be discussed with the inquirers and sponsors beforehand, and if this is culturally inappropriate for anyone, adaptations are to be made.[11]

At the conclusion of the rite, the catechumens are dismissed to ponder the readings they have just heard in the Liturgy of the Word. During the Rite of Acceptance, the dismissal occurs after the Intercessions for the Catechumens and the Prayer over the Catechumens. At most other liturgies, it will take place after the homily and before the Creed. The dismissal should be part of every liturgy the catechumens attend until they are initiated.

The words used in the dismissal can catechize the faithful about the meaning of their Baptism and the responsibilities of the baptized, who have put on Christ. In intercessory prayer, the faithful take on the priestly role of Christ to intercede with the Father for the needs of the world. In the Eucharistic Prayer, the faithful participate in the eternal prayer of thanks and praise of Christ to the Father; in Holy Communion, they receive the Lord to whom they have been eternally joined; at the dismissal they are sent out to live the Gospel in word and deed. The catechumens are preparing for these duties. The rest of the members of the assembly should be reminded of the dignity that is theirs and rejoice with those who are preparing to share in that dignity. A paragraph in the bulletin or a few words in the homily could remind parishioners of the purpose of the dismissal.

> God showers his grace on the candidates, since the celebration manifests their desire publicly and marks their reception and first consecration by the Church.
>
> —*Rite of Christian Initiation of Adults*, 41

Several optional rites may be added to the Rite of Acceptance under certain circumstances: an exorcism and renunciation of false worship (which is rarely used), the taking of a new name, the presentation of a cross, and the presentation of a Bible. When preparing the rite, consideration should be given to the many symbolic actions that already are part of the rite. Some of

---

11. RCIA, 33 §3.

the optional rites might be adapted for use at another time, such as a cate-chetical session or a Celebration of the Word for the catechumens.

The following outline may help visualize the flow of the rite:

Receiving the Candidates

- Greeting

- Opening Dialogue

- Candidates' First Acceptance of the Gospel

- Affirmation by the Sponsors and the Assembly

- Signing of the Candidates with the Cross

  ▫ Signing of the Forehead

  ▫ Signing of the Other Senses (Optional)

- Concluding Prayer

- Invitation to the Word of God

Liturgy of the Word

- Instruction

- Readings

- Homily

- Presentation of a Bible (Optional)

- Intercessions for the Catechumens

- Prayer over the Catechumens

- Dismissal of the Catechumens

Date and Time

The Rite of Acceptance may be celebrated at any time of the year. Most par-ishes celebrate it at a Sunday Mass, acknowledging that "the initiation of adults is the responsibility of all the baptized."[12] If necessary, it also may be celebrated at other times, within or outside Mass, with some or all of the community present.[13] Although it is not prohibited, most parishes find it better to avoid celebrating the rite on the Sundays of Lent and Advent.

---

12. RCIA, 9.
13. RCIA, 45.

The rite presumes that the time between Acceptance and full initiation will be "an extended period."[14] The bishops of the United States have directed that this period "should extend for at least one year."[15]

It may be helpful for pastors or other initiation ministers to reserve two or three Sundays as possible times to celebrate this rite.[16] These dates may be selected for the appropriateness of the prescribed Scripture readings and their availability on the parish calendar. If there are inquirers ready to become catechumens as a reserved date draws near, scheduling is done; if not, the date can be removed from the calendar.

Ministers of the Liturgy

When the Rite of Acceptance into the Order of Catechumens is celebrated within Mass, a priest presides; if it is celebrated outisde Mass, a priest or deacon may preside.[17] If possible, the celebrant should already be acquainted with the inquirers and their sponsors.

A full complement of ministers—readers, cantor and other musicians, and servers—should be present at this liturgy. This is an important occasion in the life of the Church and in the relationship between the Lord and those who are to become catechumens. If the liturgy is not part of a regular parish Mass, servers, readers, cantors, and other musicians will need to be recruited. All ministers should be informed that the liturgy will be somewhat different from the usual and be prepared to take their part in it.

> The term "catechumen" should be strictly reserved for the unbaptized who have been admitted into the order of catechumens.
>
> —*National Statutes for the Catechumenate*, 2

Sponsors also have an active part in this rite, and they should be prepared for it. The sponsors should be given an explanation of what will be expected of them and, if possible, walked through the rite. If they will be signing the inquirers with the Sign of the Cross, they should be shown how to do it.

As paragraph 42 of the rite notes, the inquirers should also be instructed about the rite. They should be prepared to answer the questions that will be asked and given a general understanding of how the rite will progress, but

---

14. RCIA, 75.
15. *National Statutes for the Catechumenate* (NS), 6.
16. RCIA, 18.
17. RCIA, 45.

they should not have to be concerned with where they need to be and when. The sponsors and other ministers of the rite should lead them through it.

Parishioners should be well aware that the rite will occur at the Mass. In the weeks prior to the rite, announcements could be made and also notices placed in the bulletin. On the day of the Rite of Acceptance, ushers and ministers of hospitality could alert members of the assembly as they enter the church that something special is occurring at this liturgy. If there are worship aids, they should be sure everyone receives one. These ministers can also help with the movement in and out of the church by making sure that doors are open and there are no obstacles in the way.

With so many people involved in a rite with a lot of movement, it may be helpful for someone to unobtrusively shepherd the various participants through the liturgy. A liturgy coordinator, master of ceremonies, adult server, or the initiation director might undertake the task.

Music for the Rite

Some hymnals have music for the rites of initiation, and most of the Catholic liturgical music publishers have collections for this purpose. Appropriate music that is already part of the parish's repertoire also might be used. The Christian initiation coordinator should discuss the musical requirements of the various parts of the rite with the music director and ask that person to help with the selection of music.

At several places during the Rite of Acceptance, acclamations are prescribed, and at other times, they also may be appropriate. Many parishes find that singing a set of acclamations whenever this rite is celebrated helps the assembly participate more fully and interiorize the words so that they become their own. A brief rehearsal to teach or review an acclamation is especially helpful the first few times this rite is celebrated.

In addition, processions accompanied by music are part of this rite. The movement from outside the church to inside should be accompanied. The rite recommends certain psalms as options; the proper Entrance Antiphon or other Entrance Song of the day may be appropriate. The departure of the catechumens after they are dismissed also requires processional music. A refrain that echoes the celebrant's words of dismissal, "Catechumens, go in peace, and may the Lord remain with you," might be appropriate. It may also be appropriate to repeat the antiphon of the Responsorial Psalm.

Environment for the Rite

The Rite of Acceptance requires little of the liturgical environment. The place where the initial gathering takes place might be made a bit more festive than usual with banners or greenery. The church should be decorated appropriately for the time of the liturgical year. Care should be taken that nothing obstructs movements during the numerous times in the rite when people move or stand in various places. If the catechumens will be presented with crosses or Bibles during this rite, the table on which they will rest beforehand might be decorated to harmonize with the rest of the environment and located in a conspicuous place.

Preparing the Assembly

The Rite of Acceptance, like the entire initiation process, belongs to the whole parish. For the assembly to celebrate it fully, consciously, and actively, they will need to have an understanding of the rite and know who the inquirers are and the meaning of the various symbols of the rite. They also need help in understanding what this rite means for them. Assist them with connecting to the signing of the senses by evoking the many times they as Catholics sign themselves or are signed. Most especially recall when they signed their children or godchildren at their Baptisms and make the connection between that ritual moment in the Baptism of

Help the parish understand the Rite of Acceptance by drawing a parallel with the signing of the senses and the parent signing the baby at Baptism.

children and the signing at the Rite of Acceptance, because they are the same rite. Brief explanations and questions for reflection could appear in the bulletin and other communications the weekend before the rite is celebrated and again on the weekend it is celebrated. If the catechumens agree, their pictures could be included in these announcements.

Celebrating the Rite of Acceptance into the Order of Catechumens

Receiving the Candidates

The Rite of Acceptance is the ritualization of the inquirers' movement from being observers and questioners to being publicly declared and recognized as among those in preparation for the sacraments of initiation. They move from outside to inside, from strangers to members of the household. Their presence among us is the fruit of our lives as Christians, bringing Christ to the world in the witness of our lives and in the work of evangelization. We greet them where they are and claim them for Christ before they are seated among the faithful to hear the Word of the Lord proclaimed.

> The prerequisite for making this first step is that the beginnings of the spiritual life and the fundamentals of Christian teaching have taken root in candidates.
>
> —*Rite of Christian Initiation of Adults*, 42

The rite as it is described in the ritual text is intended to take place entirely outside the church proper, ending with the entrance of the new catechumens into the church for the Liturgy of the Word. This movement from outside to inside the church is a powerful sign of what it means to be accepted as a catechumen. A liturgy held outside the church may not always be possible, however, especially if the assembly for the rite is large, as it often is when celebrated at a Sunday Mass.

The rite begins when the celebrant greets the inquirers, who have gathered at the appointed place outside the church (or inside the doors of the church) with their sponsors and other members of the faithful.[18] If the assembly consists of more than those who are gathered with the inquirers, the celebrant could begin in the church and invite those inside to accompany him to greet them. If the rite will take place at the back of the church, he or another minister may invite the assembly to turn to the back of the church. As the celebrant walks toward the inquirers, a psalm or appropriate song may be sung.

Although the rite does not mention it, the celebrant could be accompanied by ministers carrying a processional cross and, perhaps, candles (which can be a bit tricky outside). The presence of the cross is a powerful sign as the inquirers commit themselves to walk in Christ's way.

---

18. RCIA, 48.

The celebrant's greeting to the inquirers is meant to be informal and personal, expressing the Church's joy at their presence and perhaps discreetly sharing a bit of their spiritual journey to this point.

Afterward, depending on the placement of the celebrant in relation to the inquirers, the inquirers, accompanied by song, may move forward to stand in front of him. Psalm 63:1–8 is suggested for the accompanying song. In practice, this movement is rarely done.

The celebrant then introduces the inquirers to the assembly by asking each their name or by calling their names, to which they respond, "Present." The celebrant then asks the inquirers about

The Rite of Acceptance into the Order of Catechumens begins when the celebrant greets the inquirers.

their intentions in coming to the Church. The celebrant has great flexibility in how this takes place.[19] The inquirers should know that these questions will be asked; it may be helpful for their catechists or sponsors to help them consider their answers beforehand.

Candidates' First Acceptance of the Gospel

The celebrant then invites the inquirers to express their willingness to follow the way of Christ found in the Gospel. The rite suggests that the celebrant adapt this invitation to be responsive to what the inquirers have expressed in answering the previous questions. The three formularies given in the rite at RCIA, 52, are meant as models to be adapted. Many people find the formularies too wordy; an extemporaneous invitation, ending with a question that can be responded to with "I am" is appropriate in this case. The inquirers should be prepared to make that response.

On very rare occasions, it may be appropriate to replace the first acceptance of the Gospel with an exorcism and renunciation of false worship. This is to be done only with the permission of the diocesan bishop. It is primarily to be used in "regions where false worship is widespread" where one may have engaged in occult practices, such as "worshiping spiritual powers, . . . calling on the shades of the dead or . . . using magical arts."[20] It is not meant as a repudiation of other established religions the inquirer may have adhered to.

---

19. RCIA, 50.
20. RCIA, 70.

Affirmation by Sponsors and Assembly

The celebrant addresses the sponsors and assembly in his own words or those given, asking if they are ready to help those who are about to become catechumens. They answer in the affirmative. A prayer of praise follows, to which the assembly is to respond in speech or song.[21] Unless the response, which is the same as the last line of the prayer, is in the worship aid, it might help for the cantor or another minister to sing or proclaim the response and then gesture for all to repeat it.

Signing of the Candidates with the Cross

The rite envisions that the signing will take place at the same site as the earlier parts of the ritual, so do so if it is possible. This will help emphasize the symbolism of the catechumens' entrance into the church to hear the Word of God at the end of the rite.

If the place where the inquirers, ministers, and assembly have gathered does not allow everyone to see the signing of the candidates, many parishes

In many parishes, all move into the church so that the assembly will be able to see the actions of the rite.

move into the church at this point, especially if the signing of the senses will be included. Psalm 63:1–8, which was suggested earlier, or a reprise of what was sung as the celebrant approached the inquirers might appropriately accompany this movement.

The celebrant invites the inquirers and their sponsors forward for the signing.[22] If everyone has just entered the church from outside, wait until all are seated and settled. In that case, it may also be better for the inquirers and sponsors to wait in the back of the church until they are called forward.

When preparing this liturgy, consider where the inquirers and sponsors will stand for the signing. The signing is a powerful symbol not only for the individual, but for the whole assembly. Depending on the size and configuration of the church, the inquirers may be placed across the front of the church, facing the assembly; they might also be placed in the aisles, some

---

21. RCIA, 53.
22. RCIA, 54.

Depending on the size and configuration of the church, the inquirers may be placed across the front of the church, facing the assembly; they might also be placed in the aisles, some near the front of the church, some closer to the back, so that all the members of the assembly can see this important action.

near the front of the church, some closer to the back, so that all the members of the assembly can see this important action.

If there are only a few inquirers, the celebrant signs the forehead of each, repeating the given formula for each; if they are placed around the church, he may go to each one. Each sponsor then signs his or her inquirer as well, if there will be no further signings. If there are many inquirers, they take their places with their sponsors. The celebrant says a few words of explanation, then makes the Sign of the Cross over them while saying the formula as the sponsor or catechist signs them on the forehead.[23]

An acclamation is sung after each signing; the rite suggests "Glory and praise to you, Lord Jesus Christ," for which most parishes will already have a musical setting, since it is one of the Lenten Gospel acclamations. Another appropriate acclamation may be used.

If the senses are also to be signed,[24] the celebrant speaks the formula for each sense as the sponsor or catechist does the signing. The acclamation is sung after each signing. The signing concludes with the celebrant making the Sign of the Cross over the candidates, individually or all at once, while saying, "I sign you with the sign of eternal life in the name of the Father, and

---

23. RCIA, 55.
24. RCIA, 56.

During the signing of the senses, the celebrant speaks the formula for each sense as the sponsor or catechist signs the inquirer.

of the Son, and of the Holy Spirit." The new catechumens reply, "Amen." A concluding prayer is prayed.

Optional Rites

The optional rites of the Giving of a New Name and the Presentation of a Cross may be included after the signings.

If a catechumen is from a culture in which non-Christian religions give a new name, he or she may wish to adopt a new name. This may be done at the discretion of the local bishop.[25] The rite is in a simple question-and-answer format and may also take place instead as part of the Preparation Rites on Holy Saturday.[26] It is not commonly celebrated.

The presentation of a cross to the catechumens[27] may take place before or after the invitation to the Word of God. It seems, though, to flow more naturally from the conclusion of the signings, before the invitation. The cross is given as the celebrant says, "You have been marked with the cross of Christ. Receive now the sign of his love." The catechumen replies, "Amen."

No description of the cross is given, so it could be one that is worn around the neck or as a pin, or one appropriate for hanging on a wall or standing on a prayer table in the home. The cross should be well made and worthy to serve as a reminder of the day they were claimed by Christ as his own.

No indication is given regarding who presents the cross; it could be the celebrant, the catechist, or the sponsor. When preparing this rite, consideration must be made for where the crosses will be prior to the rite and how

If a cross is presented, it could be one that is worn or one appropriate for hanging on a wall or standing on a prayer table.

they will get to the individual who presents them to the catechumens. However the presentation is done, if it is done, it must not overshadow the signing of

---

25. RCIA, 73.
26. RCIA, 200.
27. RCIA, 74.

the person with the cross. Some parishes choose to give the new catechumens a cross in the catechetical session following the dismissal.

Invitation to the Word of God

The celebrant invites the catechumens and sponsors to the Liturgy of the Word. If they and the rest of the assembly are still outside the church, the movement into the church should be a procession, possibly led by ministers with cross and candles, and certainly accompanied by singing. The rite suggests Psalm 34 with the antiphon "Come, my children, and listen to me; I will teach you the fear of the Lord" or another appropriate song. If everyone is already in the church, the celebrant may simply invite them to take their places in the assembly. In either case, the celebrant might emphasize the significance of the catechumens now having a recognized place in the house of the church.

Liturgy of the Word

The celebrant briefly addresses the catechumens and the whole assembly to help them understand the importance of the Word of God proclaimed.[28] The readings are proclaimed in the usual manner, with a sung Responsorial Psalm and Gospel Acclamation, whether or not the celebration is part of the celebration of the Eucharist.

Readings

There are several options for Scripture readings for the Rite of Acceptance. If the rite takes place outside of Eucharist or at a Mass other than a Sunday Mass (or other Mass at which the readings are obligatory), the readings given in the *Lectionary for Mass* at number 743 may be proclaimed: Entrance into the Order of Catechumens under Ritual Masses, 1. For the Conferral of Christian Initiation. Other readings from the Lectionary may also be chosen.[29] If the rite is celebrated at a Sunday Mass or other Mass where the readings are obligatory, the readings prescribed for that Mass are proclaimed. A homily follows.

Presentation of a Bible

After the homily, the catechumens may be called forward so that a Bible (or a book containing the Gospel accounts) may be presented to them by the

---

28. RCIA, 61.
29. RCIA, 62.

The celebrant may present a Bible or a book containing the Gospel accounts to the catechumens.

celebrant. This may be a Bible that is given for each catechumen to keep, or it may be a large Bible or the *Book of the Gospels* used at Mass that is presented in a ritual manner and then reverenced by each catechumen in turn. An acclamation could accompany this action. A Lenten Gospel acclamation or a psalm antiphon that speaks of the Word of God would be appropriate choices for acclamations. This rite is optional.

Intercessions for Catechumens

The assembly then prays for the catechumens. As these prayers are prayed, the catechumens may be invited to stand facing the assembly, if they are not already in that position. These are prayers of intercession, similar in structure to the Universal Prayer, but specific in nature. A response different from that customarily used at Mass may emphasize the difference. Because intercessory prayer is the duty of the baptized, the catechumens are silent during this prayer.

If the rite is being celebrated at Mass, the Universal Prayer (Prayer of the Faithful) may be prayed after the candidates are dismissed. They may also be omitted, in which case intentions for the Church and the world are added to the intercessions for the catechumens.[30]

Prayer over Catechumens

A prayer spoken by the celebrant with hands outstretched over the catechumens concludes the intercessions and the Rite of Acceptance.[31]

---

30. RCIA, 65, 68.
31. RCIA, 66.

SECTION 1: PREPARING THE RITES FOR UNBAPTIZED ADULTS

Dismissal

If the Rite of Acceptance has been celebrated outside Mass, everyone is dismissed at this point.[32] When the Liturgy of the Eucharist is to follow, the catechumens are normally dismissed to continue reflecting on the Word of God. The catechumens and their catechist may be invited forward before the words of dismissal are spoken. They should have their coats, purses, and other belongings with them. The celebrant expresses the great joy of the rite just celebrated and dismisses the catechumens with words of peace. Two suggested formulas are given.[33] Music, preferably a refrain sung by the whole assembly, may accompany the procession out. The sponsors remain until the end of Mass and may join the catechumens at that time.

If for some reason the catechumens cannot be dismissed, they are invited to remain and gently reminded that they must await the day of their Baptism before they may participate fully at the Lord's table. A sample formula for this situation is provided.[34] Catechumens are never dismissed simply to go home.

> From this time on the Church embraces the catechumens as its own with a mother's love and concern. Joined to the Church, the catechumens are now part of the household of Christ, since the Church nourishes them with the word of God and sustains them by means of liturgical celebrations.
>
> —*Rite of Christian Initiation of Adults,* 47

Liturgy of the Eucharist

If the Eucharist follows, the Universal Prayer may be prayed. It could be introduced as a continuation of the Intercessions for the Catechumens (for example, "Let us continue to pray for the needs of the Church and the world") or it could be introduced in the usual way. As noted previously, it may also be omitted, as may the Profession of Faith.[35] (These permissions recognize that the Rite of Acceptance may take a bit more time than the ordinary Introductory Rites and allow the rite to be celebrated in an unhurried manner.) The Eucharist continues then with the Preparation of the Altar and the Gifts.

---

32. RCIA, 67D.
33. RCIA, 67A, B.
34. RCIA, 67C.
35. RCIA, 68.

Preparing the Rites Belonging to the Period of the Catechumenate

Whoever blesses others in God's name invokes the divine help
upon individuals or upon an assembled people.

—*Book of Blessings, 6*

Catholics believe that God the Father, through Christ and in the Spirit, is present and active among us in our rites and liturgies. Through the rites celebrated during the Period of the Catechumenate, God is doing something to the catechumens and to us. These rites are among the means by which God moves among and acts on us, shaping us and forming us in the journey of conversion.

The rites belonging to the Period of the Catechumenate are often referred to as the "minor rites" to distinguish them from the rites that mark the movement from one period to another. The word *minor* in this case is not meant to communicate that they are unimportant or optional. God's action among his people is never minor.

Remember that the catechumens are now "part of the household of Christ"[1]; they belong to the Church. Among other things, this means that they are called to participate in the rites of the Church, specifically the celebrations, blessings, anointings, and other rites that belong to the Period of the Catechumenate:

- Celebrations of the Word of God
- Minor Exorcisms
- Blessings of the Catechumens
- Anointing of the Catechumens
- Presentations of the Creed and the Lord's Prayer (optional)
- Rite of Sending to the Cathedral for Election by the Bishop

The majority of these rites are for celebration with the catechumens only. Minor exorcisms, blessings, and anointings are all worded for the

---

1. RCIA, 47.

unbaptized. They reflect and presume that the subjects of these rites are catechumens. The two exceptions in which others may be present are Celebrations of the Word of God and the Rite of Sending for Election.

Celebrations of the Word of God

"Among the rites belonging to the catechumenate, then, celebrations of the word of God are foremost."[2] There is an importance attached here to these celebrations. They are foremost, both in terms of their necessity and their frequency.

The wording in the minor exorcisms, blessings, and anointings makes it clear that these rites are for the unbaptized.

Elaborating on the Celebrations of the Word of God, the RCIA notes, "During the period of the catechumenate there should be celebrations of the word of God that accord with the liturgical season and that contribute to the instruction of the catechumens and the needs of the community."[3]

First, Celebrations of the Word should accord with the liturgical season. They are never celebrated outside the context of the time of the liturgical year in which they occur. This is important because, as the *Universal Norms on the Liturgical Year and the General Roman Calendar* (UNLY) reminds us, "Over the course of the year the Church celebrates the whole mystery of Christ, from the Incarnation to Pentecost Day and the days of waiting for the Advent of the Lord."[4]

Catholic liturgies and other rites are always celebrated with mindfulness of the liturgical season. Our rituals are celebrated according to a cycle, a rhythm, an annual pattern that takes us deeper and deeper into the mystery of Christ, the mystery in which the catechumens and candidates wish to participate. The liturgical year gives our rituals their framework. Over the course of the liturgical year then, the mysteries of Christ are unfolded:

- Advent and Christmas Time: the Incarnation and Manifestation of Jesus the Christ;
- Ordinary Time during Winter: the beginning of Jesus' public ministry, and the initial call to discipleship;

2. RCIA, 79.
3. RCIA, 81.
4. UNLY, 17.

- Lent, the Sacred Paschal Triduum, and Easter Time: the Life, Passion, Death, Resurrection, and Ascension of Christ, and the Sending of the Holy Spirit;
- Ordinary Time during Summer and Fall: the living out of the Christian life as disciples;
- November: the mystery of death, the end-time, and the Solemnity of Jesus Christ, King of the Universe.

Second, the liturgical year should guide these celebrations because through the seasons, the catechumens are instructed in the faith. Paragraph 75, one of the pivotal sections of the RCIA regarding the Period of the Catechumenate, notes that "a suitable catechesis is provided, . . . planned to be gradual and complete in its coverage, accommodated to the liturgical year, and solidly supported by celebrations of the word."

These Celebrations of the Word of God are to be one of the vehicles that help to facilitate the process of conversion and formation, and as such, they contribute to and in fact guide the instruction and catechesis that the catechumens and candidates receive. This is what paragraph 81 means when it states that these Celebrations of the Word are to be "held in connection with catechetical instruction."

The duration of the catechumenate will depend on the grace of God and on various circumstances.

—*Rite of Christian Initiation of Adults*, 76

Finally, these celebrations are to "contribute . . . to the needs of the community." One way that they do this is by helping the catechumens prepare to participate in the Liturgy of the Word at Sunday Mass.[5] "For in the readings, . . . God speaks to his people, opening up to them the mystery of redemption and salvation, and offering spiritual nourishment; and Christ himself is present through his word in the midst of the faithful."[6]

Here, the living Word of God is in a creative dialogue with humanity through the liturgy. This is not just a rereading of history, as if these saving acts of God happened once, never to be repeated. Rather, in the proclamation of the Word, what the Word says becomes present again, here and now. Through the Word we are in communion with God. This dialogue is ritualized for the

---

5. RCIA, 81
6. *General Instruction of the Roman Missal*, 55

catechumens and the candidates and indeed the whole assembly in the Celebrations of the Word.

All that has been said here about the Celebrations of the Word is reiterated and amplified in paragraph 82, which presents their fourfold purpose:

> The time spent in the catechumenate should be long enough . . . for the conversion and faith of the catechumens to become strong.
>
> —*Rite of Christian Initiation of Adults*, 76

- to implant in their hearts the teachings they are receiving: for example, the morality characteristic of the New Testament, the forgiving of injuries and insults, a sense of sin and repentance, the duties Christians must carry out in the world;

- to give them instruction and experience in the different aspects and ways of prayer;

- to explain to them the signs, celebrations, and seasons of the liturgy;

- to prepare them gradually to enter the worship assembly of the entire community.

Preparing a Celebration of the Word of God

Times for Celebrations of the Word of God

Given all that the RCIA says about the Celebration of the Word of God, what might be an occasion for celebrating it? A Celebration of the Word should certainly be used at every catechetical session during the catechumenate. Perhaps the best time would be at the beginning as a means to start the session.

Other gatherings of the catechumens would also present a good opportunity to celebrate the Word of God. If the catechumens are taking part in an evening at the parish or community soup kitchen, gather beforehand for a Celebration of the Word of God. Are the catechumens accompanying other parishioners to the parish's sister parish for Sunday Mass? Gather at the parish first for a brief Celebration of the Word of God before leaving together. Are the catechumens and candidates accompanying other parishioners to the nursing home at the holidays? Gather for a Celebration of the Word of God before leaving.

In short, any formal gathering of the catechumens and candidates would be an occasion for a Celebration of the Word of God. When activities are held within the context of prayer and Scripture, an understanding builds of how these activities are a response to Christ's call to conversion, and the catechumens' and candidates' relationship deepens with the parish community.

Ministers

These Celebrations of the Word may be celebrated by a priest or deacon, or by a qualified catechist or other lay minister.

Choosing Readings and Responsorial Psalms

"One or more readings from Scripture, chosen for their relevance to the formation of the catechumens, are proclaimed by a baptized member of the community."[7] These readings should be chosen carefully, depending on the occasion. If the gathering is for the weekly catechetical session, then the readings and psalms should reflect the topics of catechesis for that session. If the occasion is to take part in the parish or community soup kitchen, for example, the readings and psalms might focus on service or on how the Lord feeds and cares for us.

These readings from Scripture should be done with all the formularies that are familiar to a Liturgy of the Word: "A reading from . . ." to begin the proclamation, and "The Word of the Lord / Thanks be to God" to conclude. The readings would be proclaimed by one of the members of the initiation ministry, one of the sponsors, or another baptized person. Ordinarily, a sung Responsorial Psalm should follow each reading, the rite notes. A member of the parish's music ministry might lead these.

Music for the Celebration of the Word

Music and singing are basic elements to our Catholic rites and liturgies and so they should be part of the Celebrations of the Word. The music in the rite might take the form of a well-known opening hymn or song that can be sung either a cappella or with the help of a member of the parish music ministry who might accompany the hymn and lead the Responsorial Psalm. The liturgical time of year should be taken into account. If the parish is using a

---

7. RCIA, 87.

particular hymn or Responsorial Psalm during Masses, those might be considered if they fit with the readings.

The Homily

"A brief homily that explains and applies the readings should be given."[8] While technically a homily is reserved to the ordained deacon or priest, as with other rites of the Church (for example, blessings from the *Book of Blessings*, or rites from the *Pastoral Care of the Sick*), lay leaders may give a brief explanation of the readings. This brief explanation might help to situate the occasion within the context of prayer, applying the Word of God to the situation.

This element calls for an initiation minister who is well versed and even trained in this ministry of proclamation. Numerous commentaries on Scripture are available and would be excellent resources for members of the parish's initiation ministry.

RCIA, 85–89, provides the basic elements and outline of a Celebration of the Word of God. Notice that the format is the same as for any Liturgy of the Word that might be celebrated in or outside of Mass.

Concluding the Celebration

The Celebration of the Word may end simply, with the customary liturgical conclusion of a blessing. If an ordained minister is leading, it would be the ordinary "May almighty God bless you . . ." If a lay minister is leading, then it would be the blessing used by a lay minister, "May almighty God bless us, protect us from all evil, and bring us to everlasting life," said while making the Sign of the Cross.

However, the Celebration of the Word may conclude with a minor exorcism[9] or with a blessing of the catechumens.[10] When the minor exorcism is used, it may be followed by one of the blessings[11] or, on occasion, by the rite of anointing.[12] These other rites will be examined individually in the following section, but this statement points again to the importance of Celebrations of the Word of God. So important are these celebrations that they might be the context for all the other rites that belong to the catechumenate. In fact,

---

8. RCIA, 88.
9. RCIA, 94.
10. RCIA, 97.
11. RCIA, 97.
12. RCIA, 102–103.

paragraph 79 of the RCIA concludes that the other rites of the catechumenate are "ordinarily celebrated in conjunction with a celebration of the word."

The structure of a Celebration of the Word of God[13] is as follows:

Celebration of the Word of God

- Song

- Readings and Responsorial Psalm

- Homily

- Concluding Rites

Celebrating a Celebration of the Word of God

The model given in paragraphs 85 to 89 is quite sparse; it does not indicate all the usual elements of the Liturgy of the Word. Because one purpose of these celebrations is to prepare the catechumens to enter the assembly, it is appropriate to include these elements for completeness.

Catechumens who, moved by the holy Spirit, explicitly desire to be incorporated into the church, are by that very wish made part of it and with love and solicitude mother church already embraces them as her own.

—*Lumen gentium*, 14

Depending on the setting and the level of solemnity of the rite, the opening song may be sung while all, including the presider, are standing in their places or while the celebrant (and perhaps others) process in. The celebrant leads the Sign of the Cross and greets those gathered. A penitential act may take place, followed by a Collect.

A selected Scripture reading is proclaimed, followed by the Responsorial Psalm, preferably sung. A second Scripture reading may be proclaimed. A homily follows.

A Minor Exorcism, an exorcism followed by a Blessing, a Blessing alone, or, if the celebrant is a priest or deacon,[14] an Anointing with the Oil of Catechumens may take place.[15]

The rite concludes with a blessing and dismissal. If appropriate, a song may be sung.

---

13. RCIA, 85–89.
14. RCIA, 98.
15. RCIA, 89.

Minor Exorcisms

The *Rite of Christian Initiation of Adults* distinguishes a minor exorcism from a major exorcism. A major exorcism is a completely separate rite of the Church and is used solely in situations that the Church has determined to be cases of demonic possession. In a major exorcism, a specific demon is addressed and expelled. The purpose of the Minor Exorcisms of the catechumenate is much different.

The Minor Exorcisms of the catechumenate are signs of the redemptive mission of Christ. He came to save us from all that threatens to keep us from him and all that threatens us as his disciples. There is much in life today that threatens to keep us from Christ: sin, selfishness, greed, the pursuit of power and prestige, a disregard for the poorest and weakest among us. These are all things that threaten to keep us from Christ. Recall, however, in the signing in the Rite of Acceptance into the Order of Catechumens, the words "Receive the cross on your forehead. It is Christ himself who now strengthens you with the sign of his love." The Minor Exorcisms are an extension of that strengthening.

The Minor Exorcisms are "composed in the form of petitions directly addressed to God. They draw the attention of the catechumens to the real nature of Christian life, the struggle between flesh and spirit, the importance of self-denial for reaching the blessedness of God's kingdom, and the unending need for God's help."[16]

The RCIA contains the texts of the various prayers of exorcism. Eleven formularies are given asking God to perform various actions for the catechumens: for example, asking God to protect them from the spirit of evil, guard them against sin (A), remove hesitation in faith (B), remove from them the snares of the world—love of money, hatred, quarreling (B), greed (C), lust and pride (D), weakness (G), fatigue, and loss of hope (H).[17]

> The catechumenate . . . is not merely an exposition of dogmatic truths and norms of morality, but a period of formation in the entire christian life, an apprenticeship of suitable duration, during which the disciples will be joined to Christ their teacher. The catechumens should be properly initiated into the mystery of salvation and in the practice of evangelical virtues, and they should be instructed into the life of faith, liturgy, and charity of the people of God by successive sacred rites.
>
> *Ad gentes*, 14

---

16. RCIA, 90.
17. RCIA, 94.

Having asked for what is harmful to be removed, the prayers request that God may provide for, or strengthen, the good: a spirit of faith, reverence, patience, hope (B); open hearts to understand the Gospel (C); help in finding blessings in poverty, hunger, mercy, and purity of heart; endurance in persecution (D), that with hope, they may join God's priestly people (H).

As noted previously, the Minor Exorcisms ordinarily take place in a Celebration of the Word of God, immediately preceding the Final Blessing, as part of the Concluding Rite. For a special need, however, they may be prayed privately for individual catechumens. They also may be part of an Anointing of Catechumens.

Ministers, Times, and Places of a Minor Exorcism

The ordinary minister of the Minor Exorcisms is a priest, deacon, or a qualified catechist appointed by the bishop for this ministry.[18] The place would be the parish church or a chapel. The rite also notes that the Minor Exorcisms can be celebrated in the place where the catechumens normally gather and that they might even be celebrated as part of the catechetical gatherings. If this takes place, it would make sense that the exorcism would be part of the Celebration of the Word of God at the beginning of the catechetical session.

Whenever the Minor Exorcisms are celebrated, the catechumens are called to bow their heads or to kneel before the presiding minister, who extends hands over them and prays the Prayer of Exorcism.

The structure of a Minor Exorcism is as follows:

Minor Exorcism

- Prayers of Exorcism
- Catechumen bows head or kneels before celebrant (priest, deacon, or qualified catechist)
- Celebrant, with hands outstretched, prays the text of one of the eleven prayers provided (A–K)
- Catechumen responds, "Amen."

---

18. RCIA, 91. "'Not only priests and deacons, but also catechists delegated to do so may celebrate the minor exorcism and bless the catechumens (RCIA 48, 109, 119)' [RCIA 16, 91, 96, in the 1988 text, currently in use]. In the United States, delegation to perform the rite is assumed in the delegation to perform the ministry of catechist." Secretariat, Bishops' Committee on the Liturgy, *Christian Initiations of Adults: A Commentary,* Study Text 10 (Washington, DC: Office of Publishing and Promotion Services, United States Catholic Conference, 1985), p. 49.

Blessings of the Catechumens

The blessings of the catechumens are a sign of God's love and of the Church's tender care. They are bestowed on the catechumens so that, even though they do not as yet have the grace of the sacraments, they may still receive from the Church courage, joy, and peace as they proceed along the difficult journey they have begun.[19]

After the prayer of blessing, the celebrant lays hands on the catechumens.

The *Book of Blessings*, an official ritual book of the Catholic Church, offers a wonderful insight into the Catholic understanding of blessings: "Whether God blessed the people himself or through the ministry of those who acted in his name, his blessing was always a promise of divine help, a proclamation of his favor, a reassurance of his faithfulness."[20] Looking at the catechumens, all of these are elements of God's love and care that are given by the Church to strengthen them in their journey of conversion and their developing faith.

"Blessings are signs that have God's word as their basis and that are celebrated from motives of faith."[21] For this reason, as already noted, Celebrations of the Word of God would be a most opportune time to celebrate a Blessing of the Catechumens. Nine formularies are given for the Prayer of Blessing and may be chosen to connect in some way to the Celebration of the Word in which they are prayed.

As with the Word of God, blessings are meant to stir in us remembrance of all the good that God has bestowed upon us throughout history. This stirring of memory prompts us to ask in faith for more. Blessings, then, are an act of faith—an act of faith for the Church and an act of faith for the catechumens.

> Catechumens should be encouraged to seek blessings and other suffrages from the Church, since they are of the household of Christ.
>
> —*National Statutes of the Catechumenate*, 8

---

19. RCIA, 95.
20. *Book of Blessings*, 6.
21. *Book of Blessings*, 10.

Blessings are given by a priest, a deacon or, as with the Minor Exorcisms, by a qualified and trained catechist who has been appointed by the bishop.[22] The presiding minister extends hands over all the catechumens together and prays the blessing aloud. If possible, the catechumens then come before the minister who lays hands in silence on each of the catechumens individually.

Like the Minor Exorcisms, Blessings, in addition to being part of a Celebration of the Word, may be celebrated as part of a catechetical gathering or during any time that the catechumens gather formally. For special reasons or needs, they also may be celebrated privately.

The structure of the Blessing is as follows:

Blessing of the Catechumens

- Prayer of Blessing
- Celebrant (priest, deacon, qualified catechist) stretches hands over the catechumens
- Celebrant says one of five blessings, 67A–I
- Celebrant extends hands over all the children and, if appropriate, lays hands on them individually

Anointing of the Catechumens

In both the Christian and Jewish traditions, those who were anointed would be vehicles of God's presence and action in the world: priests, prophets, and kings. On Holy Saturday night, these catechumens will be vehicles for God's presence and action in the midst of the People of God in parishes around the world. The Anointing of the Catechumens helps prepare them for this.

The Rite of Blessing of Oils, used at the Chrism Mass, tells us that "by the oil of catechumens the effect of the baptismal exorcisms is extended. Before they go to the font of life to be reborn, the candidates for baptism are strengthened to renounce sin and the devil."[23] The RCIA similarly gives special attention to anointing with the oil of catechumens. It "symbolizes their need for God's help and strength so that, undeterred by the bonds of the past and overcoming the opposition of the devil, they will forthrightly take the step of professing their faith and will hold fast to it unfalteringly throughout their lives."[24]

---

22. RCIA, 96.
23. Rite of Blessing of Oils, 2.
24. RCIA, 99.

The Anointing of the Catechumens takes place primarily as part of the conclusion to a Celebration of the Word of God, but may be conferred privately for pastoral reasons.[25] These anointings can take place several times during the course of the catechumenate,[26] whenever it might seem beneficial to the catechumens. The celebrant of this anointing is a priest or deacon.[27]

The first part of the Anointing is a prayer of exorcism, asking that the catechumens be strengthened in the face of whatever threatens to keep them from Christ. The single prayer provided for the anointing of catechumens is drawn from the Gospel according to Luke, when Jesus enters the synagogue in Nazareth and reads from the scroll of the prophet Isaiah: "The Spirit of the Lord is upon me, because he has anointed me to bring glad tidings to the poor" (Luke 4:18). However, any of the Prayers of Exorcism given at paragraph 94 may be used.

> The Church, like a mother, helps the catechumens on their journey by means of suitable liturgical rites, which purify the catechumens little by little and strengthen them with God's blessing.
>
> —*Rite of Christian Initiation of Adults*, 75 §3

If the oil to be used is not that which was blessed by the bishop at the Chrism Mass, a priest, for pastoral reasons, may bless oil to be used immediately for the anointing. In this case, this prayer of blessing replaces the initial exorcism. A deacon cannot bless the Oil of Catechumens.[28]

The minister prays the Prayer of Anointing once over all the catechumens, who answer "Amen." The minister then goes to each catechumen and anoints him or her on the breast

A priest or a deacon can anoint the catechumens.

or on both hands. Traditionally, anointing the catechumens on the breast was a sign and symbol of the protection the anointing gives them, a visual allusion to armor, or a breastplate. That allusion can be lost today since such

---

25. RCIA, 100.
26. RCIA, 100.
27. RCIA, 98.
28. RCIA, 101.

protection is no longer worn. For that reason, anointing both hands might be the better pastoral choice.

The RCIA notes that the anointing might be given, "if this seems desirable, even on other parts of the body."[29] In some parishes, the forehead is anointed. In order to leave the anointing of the forehead for Holy Saturday night, when the neophytes will be anointed on the forehead with chrism in their Confirmation, perhaps the two hands still seem the better choice.

After the catechumens are anointed, one of the options for the Blessing of Catechumens may be prayed over them. If this takes place within a Celebration of the Word of God, it would be followed by the final blessing of all who have gathered.

The structure for the Anointing is as follows:

Anointing of Catechumens

- Prayer of Exorcism or Blessing of Oil
- If the celebrant (deacon or priest) is using blessed oil, prayer 102A is used.
- If the celebrant is blessing oil, prayer 102B is used.
- Anointing.
- The celebrant faces the catechumens and says the words of anointing.
- Catechumen responds, "Amen."
- The celebrant anoints each catechumen on both hands.
- The anointing may be followed by a blessing.

Presentation of the Lord's Prayer and the Creed

Though the *Rite of Christian Initiation of Adults* allows for these rites to be anticipated in the Period of the Catechumenate, it also notes that they "normally take place during Lent."[30] For this reason, they will be treated in this book when the rites of the Period of Purification and Enlightenment are addressed.[31]

---

29. RCIA, 103.
30. RCIA, 104.
31. See pages 58–77.

Preparing the Rite of Sending Catechumens for Election

The Rite of Sending the Catechumens for Election is an optional rite, and it is particular to the Church in the United States. It takes place at the end of the Period of the Catechumenate and is used as a means for the local parish community to take a particular part in the process of the catechumens being elected for full initiation at the next Paschal Vigil. The Catholic bishops of the United States approved this rite since the majority of the parish community will not go to the cathedral for the Rite of Election. For this reason, the Rite of Sending for Election closely resembles the Rite of Election itself, and it gives "the local community the opportunity to express its approval for the catechumens and to send them forth to the celebration of election assured of the parish's care and support."[32] In reality it is a wonderfully pastoral adaptation by the bishops of the United States.

Normally the Rite of Sending takes place on the First Sunday of Lent, or whenever the catechumens are to go to the cathedral for election. This may vary from diocese to diocese in the United States.

The election of the catechumens is, the Rite reminds us, the "focal point of the Church's concern for the catechumens."[33] For this reason, the opportunity for the parish to express its judgment as to the progress and the readiness of the catechumens is important.

Discernment is presumed to have taken place since, as the rite states, "the Church judges their [the catechumens] state of readiness and decides on their advancement toward the sacraments of initiation. Thus the Church makes its 'election,' that is, the choice and admission of those catechumens who have the dispositions that make them fit to take part, at the next major celebration, in the sacraments of initiation."[34]

Day and Time of the Celebration

While the Rite of Sending Catechumens for Election may take place at a Celebration of the Word of God,[35] it is most commonly celebrated at Sunday Mass on the day that the catechumens will go to the diocesan Rite of Election. Depending on when the Rite of Election is to take place or the distance to

---

32. RCIA, 107.
33. RCIA, 107.
34. RCIA, 119.
35. RCIA, 109.

the cathedral or another place where election is to be celebrated, the Rite of Sending could be celebrated on an earlier day.

Scripture Readings

When the Rite of Sending is celebrated on the First Sunday of Lent, the Scripture readings are those of the day. Should the rite be celebrated on another day, the day's Scriptures are used when they are appropriate. If those Scriptures are not appropriate, the readings of the First Sunday of Lent or other suitable readings should be selected.[36]

The Book of the Elect

The signing of the Book of the Elect is a profound yet simple moment. Like many of our liturgical symbols, such as breaking bread or pouring water, it takes an everyday action as a symbol of profound meaning. The ordinary act of signing one's name becomes a sign of the desire to enter fully into the life of the Church through the Easter sacraments.[37]

The book may be signed during the Rite of Sending and presented to the bishop at the Rite of Election or signed at the cathedral as part of the Rite of Election, depending on the practice in the diocese. RCIA, 113, notes that the catechumens may sign the Book of the Elect after the Rite of Sending. Unless the signing by the catechumens presents an undue burden on the liturgy (that is, an extraordinary number of catechumens), there seems no reason for the book to be signed later.

The signing of the book is a sign of election to the Sacraments of Baptism, Confirmation, and Eucharist. Those who are already baptized, even if they have not received all the sacraments of initiation, are already elect, as their Baptism demonstrates. They should not sign the Book of the Elect, although the practice in some dioceses may differ.

The Book of the Elect should be substantial and well made, decorated appropriately but not ostentatiously, as all liturgical objects should be. Over the years this book becomes a reminder of the journeys of faith of those who have been elected and part of the faith story of the community and the larger Church.

---

36. *Lectionary for Mass*, 744.
37. RCIA, 132.

Consider where the signing of the book will take place. It may be held by an initiation minister as the catechumen signs, or set on a small table or podium, simply decorated. The signing should not take place on the altar.

Placement of the Celebrant and Catechumens

When the catechumens are called forward, they are to stand before the celebrant. Consider having the catechumens stand facing the assembly, perhaps standing on a step, with their godparents behind, so that they can be seen by the whole assembly. The celebrant could stand at the head of the aisle and face the catechumens when addressing them and then turn to the assembly. The exact placement will depend on the configuration of the church and the number of catechumens to be sent for election, but keep in mind that the assembly should be looking at the front of the catechumens.

The structure of the Rite of Sending Catechumens for Election is as follows:

Rite of Sending Catechumens for Election

- Presentation of the Candidates
- Affirmation by the Candidates [and the Assembly]
- Intercessions for the Catechumens
- Prayer over the Catechumens
- Dismissal

Celebrating the Rite of Sending for Election

Presentation of the Catechumens

After the homily, an appropriate minister, such as the coordinator of initiation ministry, presents the catechumens to be sent for election to the celebrant. The rite provides a formula with which to present them, noting that the catechumens have progressed in their formation and conversion and attesting that they are ready to be sent to the cathedral. This presentation may be adapted and personalized according to the specific circumstances of the catechumens.

The celebrant then calls the catechumens by name to come forward with those who will be their godparents. They come forward to stand before the celebrant.

Affirmation by the Godparents (and the Assembly)

The celebrant first addresses the people, reminding them of their responsibility in assessing the readiness of the catechumens. He then turns to the godparents, who to some degree represent the rest of the people of the parish, and asks for their testimony as to the readiness of the catechumens. He asks

whether the catechumens have "taken their formation in the Gospel and in the Catholic way of life seriously," whether they have "given evidence of their conversion by the example of their lives," and whether the godparents judge them "to be ready to be presented to the bishop for the rite of election."[38] To each of these questions, the godparents are expected to answer in the affirmative.

The celebrant may turn to the assembly and ask for their approval of the catechumens. This can be a powerful way for the people of the parish to claim their responsibility in the progress of formation and conversion of the catechumens. It reminds us that "the people of God, as represented by the local Church,

If a large number of catechumens are to sign the Book of the Elect, it may be appropriate for the assembly to sing a refrain or acclamation that expresses the weight of what is occurring at this moment.

should understand and show by their concern that the initiation of adults is the responsibility of all the baptized."[39]

This might be done by the celebrant saying, "People of St. N. Parish, I now ask you: Do you judge these catechumens, with whom you have walked during their formation and conversion, to be ready to be presented to the bishop for election?" The people would then respond, "We do."

The celebrant then turns back to the catechumens and declares that the parish community has judged them ready and recommends them to the bishop to be elected in the name of Christ.

The Book of the Elect may be signed at this point. If a large number of catechumens are to sign the Book of the Elect, it may be appropriate for the assembly to sing a refrain or acclamation that expresses the weight of what is occurring at this moment. If such an acclamation or refrain was used

---

38. RCIA, 112.
39. RCIA, 9.

At the conclusion of the intercessions, the priest prays over the catechumens.

during the Rite of Acceptance into the Order of Catechumens, consider repeating it here. It creates a thread that connects the rites.

Intercessions for the Catechumens and Prayer over the Catechumens

The whole assembly then prays for the catechumens in the intercessions. Although the rite provides texts that can be used in the intercessions, it also notes that these texts may be personalized or otherwise adapted to fit various circumstances. The intercessions conclude with the Prayer over the Catechumens, which the celebrant prays with hands outstretched over the catechumens.

If the liturgy is to continue with the Eucharist, the catechumens are dismissed in the usual manner. If not, all are dismissed.

When the Eucharist does follow in the liturgy, the Universal Prayer may follow, or it may be omitted. If the Universal Prayer is omitted, the intercessions for the Church and the world would have been included in the intercessions for the catechumens. The Mass would continue with the Creed, although for pastoral reasons, it too may be omitted. The Preparation of the Altar and the Gifts follows as usual.[40]

---

40. RCIA, 117.

Preparing the Rites Belonging to the Period of Purification and Enlightenment

This is a period of more intense spiritual preparation, consisting more in interior reflection than in catechetical instruction, and is intended to purify the minds and hearts of the elect as they search their own consciences and do penance.

—*Rite of Christian Initiation of Adults*, 139

The Period of Purification and Enlightenment is the time of final preparation for those who have been elected for the Easter sacraments. If there are catechumens who have not yet been elected, they continue with their usual catechetical formation. For the elect, however, this is a time of spiritual preparation, more like a retreat than catechesis. This preparation is largely liturgical, with Scrutinies celebrated on three Sundays of Lent, the Presentations of the Creed and the Lord's Prayer during weekday liturgies, and the Preparation Rites on Holy Saturday.

For both the elect and the local community . . . the Lenten season is a time for spiritual recollection in preparation for the celebration of the paschal mystery.

—*Rite of Christian Initiation of Adults*, 138

The Scrutinies help the elect prepare to renounce sin and evil and profess faith in the Triune God at their Baptism. The Presentations prepare the elect to take their place among the baptized and to keep the faith they profess and their relationship to God as adopted children through Baptism always in their hearts and on their lips. The Preparation Rites ready the elect to profess their faith and to hear the Word of God.

The Period of Purification and Enlightenment customarily coincides with Lent, the time when the faithful prepare to renew their baptismal covenant. The Scrutinies that take place during this period help the faithful reflect on sin in their lives and renew their covenant relationship with God. They are a good preparation for the baptized to celebrate the Sacrament of Penance.

The Scrutinies

The Scrutinies are rites of self-searching and repentance. They have, above all, a spiritual purpose: "to uncover, then heal all that is weak, defective, or sinful in the hearts of the elect; to bring out, then strengthen all that is upright, strong, and good. For the Scrutinies are celebrated in order to deliver the elect from the power of sin and Satan, to protect them against temptation, and to give them strength in Christ."[1]

These are rites of purification in which the Church asks for strength for the elect as they enter into the final preparation for Baptism, Confirmation, and Eucharist. They help the elect achieve the "intimate knowledge of Christ and his Church" needed for the sacraments of initiation, and help the elect progress in genuine self-knowledge through serious examination of their lives and true repentance.[2] This self-examination is progressive, and it deepens with each Scrutiny, which is

The text of the Scrutinies speaks of the Baptism of the elect, making it clear that these rites are only for the unbaptized.

why there are three and why all three are required. No one but the bishop has the authority to permit the omission of the Scrutinies, and only then for a "serious reason" or "extraordinary circumstances."[3]

Through this progressive self-examination and deepening self-knowledge, the elect gradually learn about the mystery of sin and increase their desire to be delivered from it. As this desire increases, their spirit is filled more and more with Christ the Redeemer, who is the one to deliver them from sin. "These rites, therefore, should complete the conversion of the elect and deepen their resolve to hold fast to Christ and to carry out their decision to love God above all."[4]

1. RCIA, 141.
2. RCIA, 142.
3. RCIA, 20.
4. RCIA, 141.

The Scrutinies are prescribed solely for the unbaptized. Their status is reflected in the words of the prayers of the Scrutinies, which reference the elect and their approaching Baptism.

The readings for the Scrutinies are always those of the Third, Fourth, and Fifth Sundays of Lent for Year A. The very heart of the rites of the Scrutiny is the proclamation of the three Gospel readings from St. John: the woman at the well, the man born blind, and the raising of Lazarus. The use of these Gospel accounts in the preparation of those to be baptized dates to the fourth and fifth centuries. In their proclamation, these readings act as a beacon to shine on and illumine the lives of the elect. The light of these Gospel accounts reveals specifically how the elect need the life-giving water of Christ, where they are blind and need the light of Christ so that they may see the truth, and where they experience death in their lives and need the new life to which Christ calls them.

> The scrutinies are meant to uncover, then heal all that is weak, defective, or sinful in the hearts of the elect; to bring out, then strengthen all that is upright, strong, and good.
>
> —*Rite of Christian Initiation of Adults*, 141

While the light of these Gospels "uncover[s], then heal[s] all that is weak, defective, or sinful in the hearts of the elect,"[5] that same light reveals to the elect Christ as the only one who can give them the water of new life, the light of salvation, life in the face of death. In short, these readings reveal to the elect and to the faithful Christ as the only Savior and Redeemer.

The Scrutinies include exorcisms that address the reality that sin and evil can, in fact, keep us from Christ. These rites are meant to reveal to the elect both where in their lives they need to be purified and the goodness they possess in God.

The structure of the rite for the Scrutinies is as follows:

Liturgy of the Word
- Readings
- Homily
- Invitation to Silent Prayer
- Intercessions for the Elect
- Exorcism
- Dismissal of the Elect

---

5. RCIA, 141.

Preparing the Scrutinies

When

The three Scrutinies are celebrated on the Third, Fourth, and Fifth Sundays of Lent, at Sunday Mass.[6] For pastoral reasons, they may be celebrated on other Lenten Sundays or even during the week. In the rare and unusual circumstance of the period of Purification and Enlightenment taking place outside Lent, the three Scrutinies are celebrated on Sundays or even weekdays, with a week between them.

> We believe in you, Lord Jesus Christ. Fill our hearts with your radiance and make us the children of light!
> —*Rite of Christian Initiation of* Adults, 597

Texts

The propers for the three Scrutinies, found in *The Roman Missal* under Ritual Masses: 2. For the Celebration of the Scrutinies, are used whenever the Scrutinies are celebrated.[7] The first of these includes a commemoration of the godparents and a proper form of the *Hanc igitur* (Therefore, Lord, we pray) for Eucharistic Prayer I; a remembrance of the elect to be inserted in Eucharistic Prayer II; and a prayer for the faithful, that they might lead the elect by word and example, for Eucharistic Prayer III. These are for use in all three Scrutiny Masses.

Music

The rite suggests that a song may be sung at the conclusion of the Prayer of Exorcism; Psalms 6, 26, 32, 38, 39, 40, 51, 116:1–9, 130, 139, and 142 are given as examples, but other songs may be selected, particularly those that highlight forgiveness and mercy. A song at this point helps the elect and the assembly conclude this ritual with a focus on grace rather than sin.

Environment

The Lenten environment is appropriate for the Scrutinies. Those who tend to the environment should be told what is needed regarding space for the elect to kneel and for the movement of the celebrant among them.

---

6. See RCIA, 150–156, 164–170, 171–177.

7. RCIA, 146.

Celebrating the Scrutinies

Introductory Rites

The elect and their godparents may be included in the procession. If it seems appropriate, a shorter form of the Penitential Act could be used.

Homily

Guided by the readings and the liturgical texts, the homilist explains the meaning of the Scrutiny in the life of the elect and the parish's spiritual journey. After the homily, the elect are called forward with their godparents.

The homilist considers the Year A readings that have been proclaimed while explaining the meaning of the Scrutiny for both the elect and the spiritual journey of the faithful.

Invitation to Silent Prayer

The celebrant addresses the assembly, asking that they pray silently "that the elect will be given a spirit of repentance, a sense of sin, and the true freedom of the children of God." The elect are invited to bow their heads or kneel. The godparents remain standing. All pray silently "for some time,"[8] that is, long enough for the assembly to settle into the silence and for them to pray.

Intercessions for the Elect

The rite provides two sets of intercessions for each Scrutiny, one that is very particular to the elect and one that is a bit wider in scope but includes the elect and references the Gospel. Many parishes adapt these intercessions to reflect issues of sin and grace raised by the elect as they prepare for these Scrutinies with their godparents and catechists. The rite allows for these prayers to be combined with the Universal Prayer of the parish community, including intentions for the Church, the world, the poor and the oppressed, and the local community. Chanting the intercessions would provide greater solemnity. If it is decided to chant them, the person writing the intercessions should collaborate with the musicians so that they might be better adapted for singing. During the

---

8. RCIA, 152.

intercessions, the elect remain kneeling (if they have been kneeling) and the godparents place their right hands on the shoulders of the elect.

Exorcism

The Exorcism consists of two prayers, one addressed to God the Father, the other addressed to Jesus Christ. With the elect still kneeling (if they have been kneeling), the celebrant prays the first prayer, with hands joined, while facing the elect. He may then lay hands on the elect individually. This should be done in silence. During this part of the rite, the whole Church prays silently but intensely that God will purify, protect, and strengthen these elect. This should be explained to the community so that they can more actively participate.

Although the rite does not mention it, some parishes ask the godparents or catechist also to lay hands. With hands outstretched, the celebrant then prays the second prayer. The exorcism may conclude with a song of praise for the forgiveness and mercy of God sung by all; the elect stand for this song.

Dismissal of the Elect

The elect and any other catechumens are dismissed in the usual way for further reflection upon the rite and to further contemplate the Word of God that they have heard.

The liturgy continues with the resumption of intercessory prayer unless the Universal Prayer was combined with the Intercessions for the Elect. The Creed may follow the Dismissal of the Elect or it may be omitted. This deviates from the

As the priest lays hands on the elect, the community prays silently that God will purify, protect, and strengthen the elect.

usual pattern of the Liturgy of the Word in which the Creed follows the homily and dismissal and precedes the Universal Prayer. The ushers, music ministers, and other ministers need to be aware of any changes, since they will affect the timing of the collection and the hymn during the Preparation of the Gifts.[9]

---

9. RCIA, 156.

The Presentations

While the Scrutinies are the most notable features of the Period of Purification and Enlightenment, the two ritual Presentations—the Creed and the Lord's Prayer—are important aspects of the enlightenment of the elect during this time. They sum up and ritualize the entire action of what has taken place during the formation of those intending to receive the initiation sacraments: their coming to know and accept the Church's teachings and their deepening faith in the one God through a relationship with Jesus Christ. These rites also prepare the elect to take their place among the faithful at worship, particularly in the celebration of the Eucharist, when they will profess the faith of the Church in the Creed and call upon God as Father, as Jesus taught his followers to do. These two actions are the privilege of the baptized.

Each of the Presentations takes place during the week following a Scrutiny. The announcements and the parish bulletin on the scrutiny Sundays should include an invitation for all to participate in the Presentations. The bulletin could include some reflection questions on phrases or sections of the Creed or the Lord's Prayer, or ask the faithful to recall times when the Creed or the Lord's Prayer gave them strength or comfort. If the parish at large is invited, the homilist should preach in a way that recognizes their presence.

> With the catechumenal formation of the elect completed, the Church lovingly entrusts to them the Creed and the Lord's Prayer, the ancient texts that have always been regarded as expressing the heart of the Church's faith and prayer.
>
> —*Rite of Christian Initiation of Adults*, 147

Although these Presentations are normally celebrated with the elect, they may be celebrated during the Period of the Catechumenate when the catechumens are judged to be ready. This anticipation is allowed for pastoral reasons: as a "rite of passage" during an extended period of the catechumenate,[10] or for reasons of time, given the shortness of the Period of Purification and Enlightenment.[11]

---

10. RCIA, 33 §6.
11. RCIA, 104.

Preparing the Presentation of the Creed

As it is described in the *Rite of Christian Initiation of Adults*, the Presentation of the Creed is quite simple. It takes place, preferably, at a weekday Mass with special assigned readings. The two defining features of the rite are the homily on "the meaning and importance of the Creed in relation to the teaching that the elect have already received and to the profession of faith that they must make at their baptism and uphold throughout their lives,"[12] and the profession of the Creed by the assembly in the presence of the elect.

The homilist should be aware of the expectation the rite places on the homily and of the assigned readings long before the day of this liturgy.

The elect should be prepared for this rite by reflecting with their sponsors, godparents, and catechists on the central aspects of the faith that are expressed in the Creed. Unfamiliar words might be pointed out and explained. A brief explanation of the rite itself and what will be asked of them is also helpful.

> The Creed, as it recalls the wonderful deeds of God for the salvation of the human race, suffuses the vision of the elect with the sure light of faith.
>
> —*Rite of Christian Initiation of Adults*, 147

The assembly should be assisted in professing the Creed in a thoughtful and well-paced manner. A worship aid with the Creed printed in sense lines with pauses indicated might be prepared. The celebrant should set a deliberate pace when leading the Creed. The point of this recitation is that the elect hear and understand what is being professed.

When the assembly professes the Creed, the elect should stand facing them. Consider where the elect will stand and how they will know where they are to go. The director of initiation, a catechist, or another person familiar with the rite might guide them at the appropriate moment.

Which Creed is used in this rite? Both the Apostles' Creed and the Nicene Creed are given as options.[13] The Apostles' Creed is essentially the sacramental formula for Baptism, and the more ancient of the two; the Nicene Creed (also called the Niceno-Constantinopolitan Creed) is more theological. It may make the most sense to use the Creed that will be professed on the Sundays of Easter Time so that the newly initiated will be able to participate

---

12. RCIA, 159.
13. RCIA, 160AB.

immediately. Whichever Creed is used in the presentation is to be memorized by the elect and recited as part of the Preparation Rites on Holy Saturday.[14]

The Presentation of the Creed does not call for the giving of a written copy of the Creed as part of the rite. Nothing should interfere with the understanding that the presentation is the recitation by the faithful. It is important, however, that the elect have copies of the Creed from which to memorize; it may be appropriate to give them a beautifully printed copy in a session after the presentation is celebrated. If the community uses both Creeds at different times of the year, catechists should explain that and provide a copy of the second Creed as well. Copies of the Creeds should reflect the translations found in the current Missal.

Date and Time

The Presentation of the Creed takes place, preferably at Mass,[15] during the third week of Lent, after the First Scrutiny has been celebrated. A regularly scheduled daily Mass, or an additional Lenten Mass, might be the best time for this celebration. If circumstances do not permit this, the presentation could take place at a Liturgy of the Word service. In either case, the presence of the community of the faithful is especially significant in this rite. The whole community should know that this event is taking place and that they are welcome and encouraged to be part of it. Because the rite includes a catechetical homily on the Creed, this liturgy might be part of a Lenten event for the whole parish based on the Creed or on particular aspects of it.

Ministers of the Liturgy

Because the rite presumes that the Presentation of the Creed takes place at Mass, the celebrant is a priest. Ideally, the priest is someone who has taken part in the formation of the elect and can speak of their growth in the faith that the community will profess in their presence. A deacon may also assist in the liturgy as usual. As at other parish liturgies, readers, servers, a cantor, and other musicians are appropriate ministers.

The Presentation takes place when the community of the faithful, led by the celebrant, professes their faith in the presence of the elect. This symbolizes that the handing on of the faith to these elect has been and continues

---

14. RCIA, 193 ff.
15. RCIA, 148, 157.

The Presentation of the Creed occurs as the faithful profess the Creed.

to be the work of the whole Church. The faithful are important ministers in this liturgy; their presence is crucial. Sponsors, godparents, family members, catechists, and other members of the faithful who have supported the elect throughout their journey to faith participate in this rite primarily as members of the assembly.

Music for the Rite

In contrast to some of the other rites of the catechumenal process, the Presentations are fairly simple, amplifying usual parts of the liturgy rather than adding new ones. This celebration should feel like it is part of the parish's celebration of Lent, rather something apart from it. The Introductory Rites should be similar to those of the Lenten Sundays, although simpler, recognizing that it is a weekday liturgy. If there is a consistent Entrance Chant used on the Sundays of Lent, it might also be appropriate in this case; alternatively, a hymn emphasizing faith would be appropriate. The prescribed Responsorial Psalm for this rite is Psalm 19:8, 9, 10, 11, with the antiphon, "Lord, you have the words of everlasting life." This same psalm is also prescribed for the Easter Vigil, after the sixth Old Testament reading, providing a lovely connection between the two rites. The verse before the Gospel is John 3:16, "God so loved the world that he gave us his Son, that everyone who believes in him might have eternal life."

The Presentation of the Creed occurs after the homily, when the assembly recites the Creed with the elect facing them. Unless the assembly is used to singing the Creed, this is best done as a recitation. There are some musical settings of this moment that might be considered, but it is important to keep in mind that this proclamation of the Creed, in particular, belongs to the whole assembly, not to a solo voice to which the assembly responds.

If this rite is celebrated at Mass, the elect are dismissed in the usual way, with the customary music used for the dismissal on Sundays. Mass then continues.

The structure of the Presentation of the Creed is as follows:

Liturgy of the Word

- Readings
- Homily
- Presentation of the Creed
- Prayer over the Elect
- Dismissal of the Elect

Celebrating the Presentation of the Creed

The Introductory Rites

The celebrant and other ministers enter as usual. The elect and their sponsors and/or godparents could be included in the procession or seated in the assembly. The Penitential Act as celebrated throughout Lent is prayed, followed by the Collect. There are no propers designated specifically for the Mass at which the Presentation of the Creed is celebrated. Those for the Lenten weekday on which the rite is celebrated are used.

> My dear friends, listen carefully to the words of that faith by which you will be justified. The words are few, but the mysteries they contain are great. Receive them with a sincere heart and be faithful to them.
>
> —*Rite of Christian Initiation of Adults*, 160

The Liturgy of the Word

The readings are proclaimed in the usual manner, with the Responsorial Psalm and Gospel Acclamation sung as usual. In place of the readings assigned for the weekday Mass, the readings are from the *Lectionary for Mass* under

Ritual Masses, I. For the Conferral of Christian Initiation, 1. Catechumenate and Christian Initiation of Adults: 748, Presentation of Creed. Unlike most weekday Masses, this Mass has both a First and Second Reading.

The homily is a pivotal element of this rite. It recounts the growth in faith of the catechumens, now elect, and looks forward to their approaching Baptism, at which they will profess this faith as the grounding aspect of their lives. It should also address the faithful who are present, preparing them to renew their commitment of faith at Easter.

The Presentation of the Creed

After the homily, the elect are called forward by the deacon or another minister. The director of initiation, a catechist, or another person familiar with the rite might guide them to where they will stand. The sponsors or godparents do not accompany them. They face the assembly and are instructed by the celebrant to listen. The celebrant then recites the first line of the Creed at a moderate pace; the entire assembly joins him in the rest of the Creed. Consider where the elect will stand and how they will know where they are to go.

Prayer over the Elect

While the elect are still in place, the celebrant invites the assembly to pray, and after a few moments of silent prayer, stretches out his hand over the elect and prays the assigned prayer.

The celebrant recites the first lines of the Creed and the assembly joins in saying the rest of the Creed.

Dismissal

If the Liturgy of the Eucharist is to follow, the elect are dismissed with their catechist or, if they are to stay, they are instructed to stay as a sign of hope. If the Eucharist is not celebrated, all are dismissed. A song may conclude the celebration.

Preparing the Presentation of the Lord's Prayer

Like the Presentation of the Creed, the Presentation of the Lord's Prayer is quite simple. It takes place, preferably, at a weekday Mass with special assigned readings. The proclamation from the Gospel of Matthew in which Jesus

The liturgy for the Presentation of the Lord's Prayer might be part of a Lenten program for the parish based on aspects of the prayer.

teaches his disciples to pray is the actual presentation. It is followed by a homily that "explains the meaning and importance of the Lord's Prayer."[16]

The homilist should be aware of the expectation the rite places on the homily and of the assigned readings long before the day of this liturgy.

Prior to the rite, the elect should be prepared for it by reflecting with their sponsors, godparents, and catechists on the meaning of the Lord's Prayer, on what it teaches us about prayer and about our relationship to God through Jesus Christ. Unfamiliar words might be pointed out and explained. A brief explanation of the rite itself is also helpful.

The Presentation of the Lord's Prayer does not call for the giving of a written copy of the prayer as part of the rite. Nothing should interfere with the understanding that the actual presentation is the proclamation of the words of the Lord. It may be appropriate to give the elect a beautifully printed copy of the prayer in a session after the presentation is celebrated.

The structure of the Presentation of the Lord is as follows:

Liturgy of the Word

- Readings
- Gospel Reading (Presentation of the Lord's Prayer:)
- Homily
- Prayer over the Elect
- Dismissal of the Elect

---

16. RCIA, 181.

SECTION 1: PREPARING THE RITES FOR UNBAPTIZED ADULTS

Date and Time

The Presentation of the Lord's Prayer takes place during the fifth week of Lent, after the Third Scrutiny has been celebrated, preferably at Mass.[17] A regularly scheduled daily Mass, or an additional Lenten Mass, might be the perfect time for this celebration. If circumstances do not permit this, the presentation could take place at a Liturgy of the Word. The whole community should know that this event is taking place and that they are welcome and encouraged to be a part of it. Because the rite includes a catechetical homily on the Lord's Prayer, this liturgy might be part of a Lenten event for the whole parish based on the Lord's Prayer or on particular aspects of it.

Ministers of the Liturgy

Because the rite presumes that the Presentation of the Lord's Prayer takes place at Mass, the celebrant is a priest. Ideally, the priest is someone who has taken part in the formation of the elect and can speak of their growth in their relationship with God and in prayer. A deacon may also assist in the liturgy as usual. As at other parish liturgies, readers, servers, cantor, and other musicians are appropriate ministers.

Sponsors, godparents, family members, catechists, and other members of the faithful who have supported the elect throughout their journey to faith participate in this rite primarily as members of the assembly.

Music for the Rite

Like the Presentation of the Creed, this celebration should feel like it is part of the parish's celebration of Lent. The Introductory Rites should be similar to that of the Lenten Sundays, although simpler, recognizing that it is a weekday liturgy. If there is a consistent Entrance Chant used on the Sundays of Lent, it might also be appropriate in this case; alternatively, a hymn emphasizing our need for God's help or another theme found in the Lord's Prayer would be appropriate. The two options for the Responsorial Psalm for this rite are Psalm 23:1b–3a, 3b–4, 5, 6, with the antiphon "The Lord is my shepherd; there is nothing I shall want" and Psalm 103:1–2, 8 and 10, 11–12, 13 and 14, with the antiphon "As a father is kind to his children, so kind is the Lord to those who fear him." The verse before the Gospel is Romans 8:15,

---

17. RCIA, 178.

"You have received the Spirit which makes us God's children, and in that Spirit we call God our Father."

If this rite is celebrated at Mass, the elect are dismissed in the usual way, with the customary music used for the dismissal on Sundays. Mass then continues as usual.

Celebrating the Presentation of the Lord's Prayer

The Introductory Rites

The celebrant and other ministers enter as usual. The elect and their sponsors and/or godparents could be included in the procession or seated in the assembly. The Penitential Act as celebrated throughout Lent is prayed, followed by the Collect. There are no propers designated specifically for the Mass at which the Presentation of the Lord's Prayer is celebrated. Those for the Lenten weekday on which the rite is celebrated are used.

The Liturgy of the Word

The First and Second Readings are proclaimed in the usual manner, with the Responsorial Psalm sung as usual. In place of the readings assigned for the weekday Mass, the readings used are in the *Lectionary for Mass* under Ritual Masses, I. For the Conferral of Christian Initiation, 1. Catechumenate and Christian Initiation of Adults: 749, Presentation of the Lord's Prayer. Unlike most weekday Masses, this Mass has both a First and Second Reading.

After the Second Reading, the elect are called forward by the deacon or another minister and stand facing the ambo. Their sponsors or godparents do not accompany them. The Gospel Acclamation is then sung. Before the proclamation of the Gospel, the celebrant instructs the elect to listen as the Lord teaches his followers how to pray, and the Gospel is proclaimed.

Note that the Lord's Prayer in the Gospel reading, Matthew 6:9–13, appears in the Lectionary in the form most commonly prayed by Catholics, which is somewhat different from most translations of the Bible.

> The Lord's Prayer fills them [the elect] with a deeper realization of the new spirit of adoption by which they will call God their Father, especially in the midst of the eucharistic assembly.
>
> —*Rite of Christian Initiation of Adults*, 147

The homily is catechetical in nature, opening up the meaning and importance of the prayer for both the elect and the faithful.

Prayer over the Elect

After the homily, while the elect are still in place, the celebrant invites the assembly to pray, and after a few moments of silent prayer, stretches out his hand over the elect and prays the assigned prayer.

Dismissal

If the Liturgy of the Eucharist is to follow, the elect are dismissed with their catechist or, if they are to stay, they are instructed to stay as a sign of hope. If the Eucharist is not celebrated, all are dismissed. A song may conclude the celebration.

Celebrating the Preparation Rites on Holy Saturday

Finally, the day of the great event, the Easter Vigil, arrives. It is a day of excitement and anticipation for the elect and their families and friends. It is also a long day. It would not be unusual for the elect to be caught up in last-minute details, such as housecleaning, shopping, or preparing Easter baskets and special foods for Easter dinner before leaving for the Vigil. Easily, day could pass into evening with the elect tired out and focused on many things.

> The elect are to be advised that on Holy Saturday they should refrain from their usual activities, spend their time in prayer and reflection, and, as far as they can, observe a fast.
>
> —*Rite of Christian Initiation of Adults*, 185 §1

The *Rite of Christian Initiation of Adults* proposes an alternative vision for the hours preceding the Easter Vigil to help the elect prepare for their initiation: "The elect are to be advised that on Holy Saturday they should refrain from their usual activities, spend their time in prayer and reflection, and, as far as they can, observe a fast."[18] Catechists could assist the elect in deciding how to the spend the day by offering spiritual materials to read, reviewing the meaning of fasting and the reason that it is a good preparation for the sacraments they are about to celebrate, and helping them find quiet times and places on a day when the church itself is likely to be full of activity.

---

18. RCIA, 185 §1.

The best way to help the elect spend at least part of the day in preparation would be for them to gather with catechists, pastors, and other members of the community who have supported them, including sponsors, godparents, family members, and friends for a time of prayer and preparation. The time together could include a simple walk through of things the elect will want to know for the evening, such as where they and their families should be seated in the church, where they will change clothes, and where they can leave their dry clothes before the liturgy begins and their wet clothes after Baptism. A brief explanation of the movements of the night's liturgy will be helpful, but a detailed rehearsal should not be necessary. Be sure to instruct the elect on how to receive the Body and Blood of Christ reverently. Assure the elect and their godparents that they will be accompanied whenever they need to move. The time together could also include a simple fasting meal, such as soup and bread, and a directive that everyone take a nap when they get home.

The most important part of the gathering, of course, is prayer. The RCIA offers suggestions for a Celebration of the Word at which one or more preparatory rites may be included:

- the Presentation of the Lord's Prayer, if it has been deferred,

- the "return" or recitation of the Creed,

- the Ephphetha Rite,

- the choosing of a baptismal name.[19]

That Celebration of the Word would be within the following model that the *Rite of Christian Initiation of Adults* provides for a Celebration of the Preparation Rites:[20]

Celebration of the Preparation Rites

- Song

- Greeting

- Reading of the Word of God

- Homily

- Celebration of the Rites Chosen

- Concluding Rites

---

19. RCIA, 185 §2.
20. RCIA, 187–192.

Readings and Homily: Each of the preparation rites has suggested readings; one or more of these readings may be chosen for proclamation. A suitable psalm or hymn may be sung between the readings if there will be more than one. A brief homily follows.

The Presentation of the Lord's Prayer: The Presentation of the Lord's Prayer, which is prescribed to be celebrated during the fifth week of Lent and may be celebrated during the Period of the Catechumenate, is also an option for the Preparation Rites if it has not yet been celebrated. The fact that the RCIA offers three opportunities for the Lord's Prayer to be presented speaks to the importance of this rite. The Lord's Prayer is the essential prayer of Christians—the foundation of all Christian prayer and the key to understanding who we are as God's children through Baptism into Christ. The newly baptized will pray the Lord's Prayer publicly with the community for the first time before they receive the Body and Blood of Christ at the Easter Vigil, at every Eucharist and celebration of the Liturgy of the Hours thereafter, and in private prayer. The opportunity to catechize about and celebrate this important prayer should not be omitted from the elect's formation.

Recitation of the Creed: The Recitation of the Creed may be celebrated if the Presentation of the Creed was celebrated earlier. This rite is also called the "return of the Creed" and demonstrates that the elect know the Creed by

The Ephphetha Rite impresses on the elect their need of grace to hear God's Word and profess it.

heart, symbolizing their reception of the Church's teachings and preparing them to profess their faith at the font through the questions of the baptismal rite and at the Eucharist when the Creed is professed by the assembly. If this rite and the Ephpheta Rite are both celebrated, the Ephphetha Rite takes place prior to the Prayer before the Recitation.[21]

Ephphetha Rite: The Ephphetha Rite is based on the healing story in Mark 7 in which Jesus opens the ears of a deaf man and cures his speech impediment. "By the power of its symbolism the Ephphetha Rite, or rite of opening the ears and mouth, impresses on the elect their need of grace in order that

---

21. RCIA, 194.

they may hear the word of God and profess it for their salvation."[22] This rite may be celebrated alone or after the Recitation of the Creed.

Choosing a Baptismal Name: The Rite of Choosing a Baptismal Name is normally not celebrated in the United States; the United States Conference of Catholic Bishops has decided that the norm in this country is that the giving of a new name is not done. The rite may be celebrated at the discretion of the diocesan bishop if the person to be baptized is from a culture in which it is the custom of non-Christian religions to do so.[23] It also is not celebrated if, at the discretion of the bishop, it took place at the Rite of Acceptance into the Order of Catechumens.[24] In both cases, the name chosen may be "either a traditional Christian name or a name of regional usage that is not incompatible with Christian beliefs."[25]

This rite is not a continuation of the practice of taking a Confirmation name, which, although it has not been part of the Confirmation Rite for decades, is still practiced in some places. If it seems appropriate, the rite may be adapted to "consist simply in an explanation of the given name of each of the elect."[26]

Concluding Rites: A blessing and dismissal conclude the Preparation Rites.[27]

Regarding Anointing on Holy Saturday

Those who have studied the third edition of *The Roman Missal* may have noticed this rubric in the section "Easter Vigil in the Holy Night," 48:

> After the blessing of baptismal water and the acclamation of the people, the Priest, standing, puts the prescribed questions to the adults and the parents or godparents of the children, as is set out in the respective Rites of the Roman Ritual, in order for them to make the required renunciation.
>
> *If the anointing of the adults with the Oil of Catechumens has not taken place beforehand, as part of the immediately preparatory rites, it occurs at this moment.*" [emphasis added]

---

22. RCIA, 197.
23. RCIA, 33 §4.
24. RCIA, 73, 200.
25. RCIA, 200.
26. RCIA, 200.
27. RCIA, 203–205.

This rubric contradicts RCIA, 33 §7:

> The National Conference of Catholic Bishops approves the omission of the anointing with the oil of catechumens both in the celebration of baptism and in the optional preparation rites for Holy Saturday. *Thus, anointing with the oil of catechumens is reserved for use in the period of the catechumenate and in the period of purification and enlightenment and is not to be included in the preparation rites on Holy Saturday or in the celebration of initiation at the Easter Vigil or at another time.* [emphasis added]

Because the decision of the National Conference of Catholic Bishops (now called the United States Conference of Catholic Bishops) was made in accord with discretionary powers that the *Rite of Christian Initiation of Adults* gives to conferences of bishops, and it was approved by the Holy See, it is particular law for the United States and is not superseded by the third edition of *The Roman Missal.* In short, in the United States, the anointing with the Oil of Catechumens is still reserved to the Period of the Catechumenate and is not done either at the Preparation Rites or at the Easter Vigil.[28]

---

28. Email response to query, Fr. Michael J. Flynn, Secretariat of Divine Worship, United States Conference of Catholic Bishops, February 11, 2016.

Preparing the Celebration of the Sacraments of Initiation at the Easter Vigil

The Easter Vigil, in the holy night when the Lord rose again, is considered the "mother of all holy Vigils," in which the Church, keeping watch, awaits the Resurrection of Christ and celebrates it in the Sacraments.

—Universal Norms on the Liturgical Year and the General Roman Calendar, 21

Of all the sacred days and seasons of the liturgical calendar, the Triduum—the Three Days, from the Mass of the Lord's Supper on Holy Thursday night through Evening Prayer on Easter Sunday—"shines forth as the high point of the entire liturgical year. Therefore the preeminence that Sunday has in the week, the Solemnity of Easter has in the liturgical year."[1] On the premier liturgy of the preeminent Sunday of the year we celebrate in a particularly festive and solemn way the Paschal Mystery of our Lord Jesus Christ. How fitting that we celebrate the sacraments of initiation by which those who have been journeying with the Church are united to his Death and Resurrection, are filled with the Holy Spirit, are participants in the sacrificial banquet celebrated for the life of the world and are sent out to bring Good News to the world.

> As proclaimed in the prayers for the blessing of the water, baptism is a cleansing water of rebirth.
>
> *—Christian Initiation, General Introduction, 5*

Preparing to Celebrate the Sacraments of Initiation

Environment

Those who will be decorating the church for the Vigil should know where the movements of the liturgy will take place. For the rites of initiation, they should know how the elect, in procession or not, will approach the font and

---

1. UNLY, 18.

Those who prepare the environment should be sure that nothing obstructs any of the movements during the Easter Vigil liturgy.

where Confirmation will take place so that the area is clear. Tables for baptismal garments, candles, and towels for those being baptized, if they are needed, should be strategically placed to be accessible but not prominent; they might be covered with white cloths for uniformity. Holders for the baptismal candles could be arranged so that they might remain burning throughout the Liturgy of the Eucharist, if this is desirable.

Areas with towels for the newly baptized to change into their dry clothes should be available. Plastic bags for wet clothes might be provided. A safe area to store dry clothes before Baptism and wet clothes afterward should be prepared.

Ministers

Minister of Confirmation: The priest or bishop who confers the Sacrament of Baptism on adults and children of catechetical age is also to be the minister of Confirmation when they are celebrated at the same rite. Any time a priest baptizes a person of catechetical age, he is to confirm that person immediately. He does not need special delegation from the bishop; the law itself gives him the faculty.[2] If a large number of candidates is to be confirmed, the minister of Confirmation may associate other priests with himself to administer the sacraments.[3]

2. See *Code of Canon Law* (CIC), cc. 883 2°, 885 §2.

3. RCIA, 14, 232.

Assisting Ministers: Initiation ministers or others could be assigned to the elect to accompany them to the various places in the liturgy that they will need to go. They could also assist with chrism, towels, baptismal garments, and candles during the baptismal rite.

For safety reasons, assistants may be needed to be prepared with towels to dry off any areas of the floor that are wet from the baptisms.

Ushers should know about and be prepared to help with the various movements of the newly baptized and the whole assembly.

The priest who baptizes an adult or child of catechetical age should, when the bishop is absent, also confer confirmation.

—*Rite of Christian Initiation of Adults*, 14

Elect

If the elect are to be baptized by immersion or the pouring of significant amounts of water, as is preferable, they may arrive at the Vigil dressed in simple clothing that they can easily change. Many parishes provide robes, usually of a dark color, for the elect to wear before and during Baptism.

The Font

> In the celebration of baptism the washing with water should take on its full importance as that sign of the mystical sharing in Christ's death and resurrection through which those who believe in his name die to sin and rise to eternal life. Either immersion or the pouring of water should be chosen for the rite . . . to ensure the clear understanding that this washing is not a mere purification rite but the sacrament of being joined to Christ.[4]

If the parish baptismal font does not accommodate Baptism by immersion or allow an adult to stand or kneel while water is poured, a temporary pool could be placed next to the font to allow water from the font to be poured over the heads of those being baptized.

Research would need to be done into what might serve as an appropriate pool. Whatever is used, it should be substantial and modestly decorated, an image of the womb of the Church from which emerges a new creation. It should not resemble a wading pool, hot tub, or a shopping-mall fountain. Even if the font is impermanent, it is an important element in a sacred action.

---

4. RCIA, 213.

Note that the *Rite of Christian Initiation of Adults* directs that the celebration of Baptism should take place within view of the assembly.[5]

Ritual Books

All of the Paschal Vigil is found in *The Roman Missal*, except for the rites of Baptism and Confirmation, which are found in the *Rite of Christian Initiation of Adults*. Be sure that both books are available and marked with ribbons in the appropriate places, and that the servers know which book is needed when.

Structure of the Service

The structure of the celebration is as follows:

Service of Light

Liturgy of the Word

Celebration of Baptism

- Presentation of the Candidates

- Invitation to Prayer

- Litany of the Saints

- Blessing of the Baptismal Water

- Profession of Faith

  □ Renunciation of Sin

  □ Profession of Faith

- Baptism

- Explanatory Rites

  □ Clothing with a Baptismal Garment (optional)

  □ Presentation of a Lighted Candle

Celebration of Confirmation

- Invitation

- Laying on of Hands

- Anointing with Chrism

---

5. RCIA, 218.

Renewal of Baptismal Promises

- Invitation

- Renewal of Baptismal Promises

  ▫ Renunciation of Sin

  ▫ Profession of Faith

- Sprinkling with Baptismal Water

Celebration of Reception

- Invitation

- Profession by the Candidates

- Act of Reception

Liturgy of the Eucharist

Celebrating the Sacraments of Initiation at the Vigil

Service of Light

The Church, including the elect, gathers at the fire. Position the elect near the fire, wearing their prebaptismal robes, if these are used, so they can fully experience this powerful symbol and so that they can be symbols of new life

Allow the elect to stand by the Easter fire so that they can experience the sign and also be signs of new life to the community.

to the rest of the assembly. Let the elect follow immediately behind the Paschal candle as it leads the assembly into the dark church. This make sense symbolically because the elect will be the ones who will be made anew tonight by passing through the waters. It also makes sense logistically: by being immediately behind the Paschal candle, they can more easily take their reserved seats as the faithful follow in behind them.

Liturgy of the Word

The Lectionary for the Paschal Vigil presents nine readings, seven from the Old Testament and two from the New

Testament. For pastoral reasons fewer Old Testament readings may be used; however, note that the Exodus reading must always be used.

Consider using all the readings, especially when there are elect to be baptized. These stories tell of God's powerful acts of salvation throughout history. This night the elect are added to this story. They are the next chapter in this great history of God's saving presence and action in the world, in our midst.

Baptismal Liturgy

Presentation of the Candidates and the Litany of the Saints: There are three options for the presentation of the candidates, depending upon the layout of each parish church and upon how the Baptisms will take place.[6]

> Our soul waits for the LORD,
>   who is our help and our shield.
> May your kindness, O LORD, be upon us
>   who have put our hope in you.
>   —Responsorial Psalm 33:20, 22

If there is to be no procession to the font, option A is used. The celebrant goes immediately to the font after the homily and the elect are called forward, together with their godparents. In this case, the invitation to prayer and the Litany of the Saints follow while all stand in their place.

When there will be a procession to the font, option B is used. It calls for the elect to process behind the deacon or other minister carrying the Paschal candle to the font. The celebrant follows the elect and godparents. During the procession, the Litany of the Saints is sung. This option suits well those churches that have a substantial font that has its own space within the church.

In deciding which option to use, consider the liturgical symbolism of a procession. It is a way of praying with our bodies, a physical enactment of our prayer. It symbolizes the great

The procession to the font symbolizes the pilgrimage the faithful make to the heavenly Jerusalem.

pilgrimage we make to the heavenly Jerusalem, the journey of faith that all make throughout our lives, including the journey that the elect have been making in the process of their conversion.

---

6. RCIA, 219.

If option B is used, once the procession reaches the font, the celebrant gives the invitation to prayer and the blessing of the water takes place immediately.

If the parish does not have a substantial font with its own space within the church, or if the font is a fixed font that is located in the sanctuary, option C, when Baptism is celebrated in the Sanctuary, can be used. A minister calls the elect forward, together with their godparents, and the invitation to prayer is given, followed by the Litany of the Saints.

Both options A and C allow for the Litany of the Saints to be sung after all the elect have been called by name, and while all of them make their way to the font. All three options call for the positioning of the candidates at the font in such a way that the full congregation might witness the Baptisms.

> May this water receive by the Holy Spirit
> the grace of your Only Begotten Son,
> so that human nature, created in
>   your image
> and washed clean through the Sacrament
>   of Baptism
> from all the squalor of the life of old,
> may be found worthy to rise to the life
>   of newborn children
> through water and the Holy Spirit.
> —Blessing of Baptismal Water, Easter Vigil

The Litany of the Saints is sung by two cantors,[7] with the assembly responding. The Litany may be expanded with additional saints' names, such as the titular saint of the church, patron saints of the elect, or others of particular importance to the community. The music director and initiation coordinator should consult with each other regarding the additional names.

When the elect have gathered around the font, the celebrant prays the Blessing of Baptismal Water.

Blessing of Baptismal Water: Once all have assembled around the baptismal font, the celebrant prays the Blessing of Baptismal Water. Option A of the Blessing of Baptismal Water[8] is prayed when there will be Baptisms. This prayer provides a long remembrance of the saving works of God

---

7. *The Roman Missal*, 41.
8. RCIA, 222.

through the element of water, concluding with a prayer for the blessing of the water by the power of the Holy Spirit, followed by an acclamation of the people. The blessing appears in *The Roman Missal* with a different translation, and either may be used.[9] Decisions about which option or translation to use rest with the celebrant and liturgy director. Music for the acclamations should be included in the worship aid for the Vigil; strong leadership by the cantor or choir will help lead the assembly in these acclamations.

Profession of Faith: There are two parts to the Profession of Faith: the renunciation of sin and the profession of faith. "The elect . . . renounce sin and Satan in order to commit themselves for ever to the promise of the Savior and to the mystery of the Trinity."[10] It is important that everyone in the church is able to hear the elect make this renunciation and profession. In their preparation, the elect might be guided in responding strongly; if needed, microphones could be used.

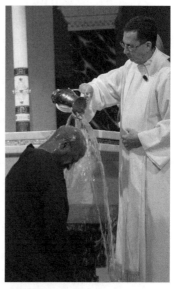

Either the translation in *The Roman Missal* or that found in the *Rite of Christian Initiation of Adults* may be used.[11]

The renunciation may be made by the elect as a group or individually.[12] The Profession of Faith is done individually, unless there are "a great many" to be baptized, when the profession may be done in a group. Each of the elect is baptized immediately after making his or her profession.[13]

Baptism: Each of the elect comes to the font for Baptism individually. If the method is by immersion, the elect steps into the font. With one

After the profession of faith, the elect come forward individually to be baptized.

or both godparents touching the elect, the priest immerses the elect three times under the water using the customary formulary: "N., I baptize you in the name of the Father," as he immerses the first time; "and of the Son," as he immerses

---

9. Letter dated November 30, 2011, by Archbishop Gregory M. Aymond, chairman of the Bishops' Committee on Divine Worship.

10. RCIA, 211.

11. Letter dated November 30, 2011, by Archbishop Gregory M. Aymond, chairman of the Bishops' Committee on Divine Worship.

12. RCIA, 224.

13. RCIA, 225.

a second time, "and of the Holy Spirit" as he immerses a third time. If the method of Baptism is to pour water over the whole body of the elect (which is still a form of immersion), the elect stands or kneels in the font as the celebrant says, "N., I baptize you in the name of the Father," as he pours water over the full body a first time, "and of the Son," as he pours water a second time, "and of the Holy Spirit" as he pours water over the full body a third time.

If Baptism is by means of infusion, where the elect approaches the font and leans his or her head over it, then one or both godparents places the right hand on the shoulder of the elect. The celebrant pours water over the forehead three times, saying the formulary as the water is poured.

An acclamation may be sung after each of the elect is baptized. An "Alleluia," one of the acclamations used during the Blessing of the Baptismal Water, or another acclamation familiar to the assembly may be appropriate; RCIA, 595, offers texts that may be used as acclamations.

No matter how the Baptisms are conferred, remember that Christ Jesus stands before us this night, alive in his new members. This is a moment of great joy for the parish community and indeed for the whole Church.

Explanatory Rites: The Explanatory Rites give expression to what has just been celebrated, to what God has just done in our midst.[14] The Anointing after Baptism, the clothing with a baptismal garment, and the presentation of a lighted candle are explanatory rites.

Anointing after Baptism: The only time the anointing with chrism takes place instead of Confirmation is if the person who has been baptized has not yet reached catechetical age. Note that this anointing is made on the crown of the head, in contrast to the anointing of Confirmation, which is made on the forehead.

Clothing with a Baptismal Garment: After all the Baptisms have taken place, an assistant may hand the white robes to the godparents. With the neophytes standing together, their godparents might step forward with white robes folded in their arms. Together the godparents hand the robes to the neophytes while the celebrant says the accompanying prayer, which notes that the neophytes have been clothed in Christ.

Presentation of a Lighted Candle: Immediately after this, the godparents are given a candle. The celebrant calls the godparents forward to light the candle from the Paschal candle. An assistant may need to take the Paschal candle from its candle stand to allow the flame to be reached. As with the

---

14. RCIA, 227.

white garment, the godparents go to the neophytes and hand them the lighted candles as the celebrant prays the accompanying prayer.

Confirmation

Confirmation is the completion of the neophytes' Baptism, the sealing of that washing with the fullness of the Holy Spirit. Having just been bap-

The Paschal candle may need to be removed from the stand for the godparent to light it.

tized, the neophytes are still standing at the font. Depending on the placement of the font, they may remain there or move to a place in the sanctuary. The priest or bishop who has conferred Baptism is also to confer Confirmation.

If a large number of people are being confirmed, the assembly may sing an appropriate antiphon or hymn. It may be best to wait until one or two people have been confirmed, so that the assembly may hear the words of the sacrament.

Invitation: The priest speaks to the newly baptized, explaining the meaning of Confirmation. He then invites the rest of the assembly to pray for the Spirit who will "anoint them to be more like Christ, the Son of God."[15] A silence of sufficient length to allow for such prayer should follow.

> The conjunction of the two celebrations [Baptism and Confirmation] signifies the unity of the Paschal Mystery, the close link between the mission of the Son and the outpouring of the Holy Spirit, and the connection between the two sacraments through which the Son and the Holy Spirit come with the Father to those who are baptized.
>
> —*Rite of Christian Initiation of Adults,* 215

Laying on of Hands and Anointing with Chrism: The priest then extends his hands over all the newly baptized and prays the prayer asking the Father to send the fullness of the Spirit upon them. Then, after being brought the chrism, and in the sight of all the people, their Baptism is confirmed as the priest anoints each neophyte on the forehead with the chrism, praying the given formulary, "N., be sealed with the Gift of the Holy Spirit." While this is being done, one or both of the godparents place the right hand on the neophyte's shoulder. If several people are being confirmed, the assembly

---

15. RCIA, 233.

The godparent's right hand is placed on the shoulder of the neophyte during the anointing with chrism at Confirmation.

may support the ritual by singing an appropriate antiphon or hymn. Once all the newly baptized are confirmed, and if they were baptized by immersion, they go to change into their white garments.

Renewal of Baptismal Promises

Invitation: The celebrant then invites the rest of the assembly to renew their baptismal promises and their Baptism through the sprinkling of the baptismal water. Before the renunciation of sin is made, the candles used at the beginning of the Vigil are relighted from the Paschal candle.

Renunciation of Sin and Profession of Faith: The priest uses the same formulary of renunciation and profession that was used for the elect.

Sprinkling with Baptismal Water: Afterward, while an antiphon or another hymn is sung, the priest sprinkles the faithful with the newly blessed baptismal water. The sprinkling should be done with deliberate and full gestures, making sure that everyone in the assembly is sprinkled. For the baptized, this is the moment to which forty days of fasting, prayer, and almsgiving has led. In many parishes, the entire assembly is invited to the baptismal font to renew their Baptism, in place of the sprinkling, although this is not men-

After the faithful renew their baptismal promises, the celebrant sprinkles them with baptismal water.

tioned in the rite. The rite prescribes the singing of the *Vidi Aquam* (I Saw Water Flowing) for the sprinkling of the people after the Renewal of Baptismal Promises; another song of a baptismal nature may be used instead.

Return of the Neophytes to the Assembly: If the neophytes left the assembly to dry off and change clothes, they should return to the assembly before the Universal Prayer. They should be wearing their white garments and carrying their lighted baptismal candles as they process in. Joyful music should accompany them as they take their places in the assembly. They may extinguish their candles or put them in a place prepared for them.

Liturgy of the Eucharist

Finally in the celebration of the eucharist, as they take part for the first time and with full right, the newly baptized reach the culminating point in their Christian initiation. In this Eucharist the neophytes, now raised to the ranks of the royal priesthood, have an active part both in the general intercessions and, to the extent possible, in bringing the gifts to the altar. With the entire community they share in the offering of the sacrifice and say the Lord's Prayer, giving expression to the spirit of adoption as God's children that they have received in baptism. When in communion they receive the body that was given for us and the blood that was shed, the neophytes are strengthened in the gifts they have already received and are given a foretaste of the eternal banquet.[16]

The rite notes a number of things about the celebration of the Eucharist at the Vigil. Even though the Litany of the Saints was prayed, the Universal Prayer is prayed so the newly baptized may take part, exercising their baptismal priesthood for the first time.[17] On this night, it is most appropriate that the newly baptized bring forth the gifts. On this night they pray the Lord's Prayer with the entire community, "giving expression to the spirit of adoption as God's children that they have received in baptism."[18]

At the Easter Vigil, it is appropriate that the newly baptized bring forth the gifts.

Special interpolations are given in *The Roman Missal* at Ritual Masses, I. For the Conferral of the Sacraments of Christian Initiation: 3. For the Conferral of Baptism, for Eucharistic Prayers I, II, and III. These interpolations reference the newly baptized and their godparents.[19] Before the Lamb of God, the celebrant may speak briefly to the newly baptized, reminding them of the preeminence of the Eucharist in their lives now that they are initiated. Finally, the Rite notes that it is most fitting for the newly baptized and newly received to come forward in the Communion

---

16. RCIA, 217.
17. RCIA, 241.
18. RCIA, 217.
19. RCIA, 242.

procession first, to receive the Bread of Life and the Cup of Salvation; that is, Communion under both kinds.[20]

Period of Mystagogy

The *Rite of Christian Initiation of Adults* refers to the newly baptized as *neophytes*, a word that comes from the Greek for "new plants." Like new plants, the neophytes need tending as they take their places as full members of the Church.

> This is a time for the community and the neophytes together to grow in deepening their grasp of the paschal mystery and in making it part of their lives through meditation on the Gospel, sharing in the eucharist, and doing the works of charity. To strengthen the neophytes as they begin to walk in newness of life, the community of the faithful, their godparents, and their parish priests (pastors) should give them thoughtful and friendly help.[21]

Now that the days of the Lord's Passion
have drawn to a close,
may you who celebrate the gladness of
the Paschal Feast
come with Christ's help, and exulting
in spirit,
to those feasts that are celebrated in
eternal joy.

—Solemn Blessing, Easter Vigil

This description of the Period of Mystagogy closely matches paragraph 75 of the RCIA, which describes the training in the Christian life that is to take place during the Period of the Catechumenate in four ways: catechesis accommodated to the liturgical year and supported by the Word of God; learning the Christian way of life from the community; celebration of liturgical rites; and participating in the apostolic life of the Church. Both paragraphs describe parish life as much as they describe periods of formation. The catechumenate, then, is the time when catechumens learn to believe and live as the Church believes and lives. The Period of Mystagogy is when they, as baptized believers, begin to live the Christian life fully, centered in personal experience of the Eucharist.

For this reason, the Sundays Masses of Easter Time are the main setting for mystagogy. "Besides being occasions for the newly baptized to gather

---

20. RCIA, 243.
21. RCIA, 244.

with the community and share in the mysteries, these celebrations include particularly suitable readings from the Lectionary, especially the readings for Year A."[22] Of course, the homilist will need to preach the Scriptures of Easter Time in light of the presence of the neophytes, but even when there are no neophytes, the Sundays of Easter are the premier time for focusing on the centrality of the Eucharist in the Christian life.

The intensity of Holy Week itself, with its Paschal Triduum, followed by the joyful celebration of fifty days that climax in Pentecost, is an excellent time for the homilist to draw links between the Scriptures and the Eucharist. It was precisely in the "breaking of the bread"—which recalled Jesus' total gift of self at the Last Supper and then upon the Cross—that the disciples realized that their hearts burned within them as the risen Lord opened their minds to the understanding of the Scriptures. A similar pattern of understanding is to be hoped for still today. The homilist works diligently to explain the Scriptures,

> Grant, we pray, almighty God,
> that our reception of this paschal Sacrament
> may have a continuing effect
> in our minds and hearts.
> Through Christ our Lord.
>
> —Prayer after Communion, Second Sunday of Easter

but the deeper meaning of what he says will emerge in "the breaking of the bread" at that same liturgy if the homilist has built bridges to that moment.[23]

In addition, the neophytes and their godparents sit together in a special place throughout Easter Time in the assembly, and prayers for them are included in the Universal Prayer.

The Second Sunday of Easter was at one time known as *Dominica in alba depositis,* signifying that the neophytes, who wore their white garments for a week after Easter while they were catechized about the meaning of the initiation rites they had experienced, set their robes aside on this day, appearing the same as the rest of the assembly. The liturgy still acknowledged their presence. The Introit, based on chapter 2 of the First Letter of St. Peter, was *Quasi modo geniti infantes, rationabile, sine dololac concupiscite.*[24] It is still

---

22. RCIA, 247.

23. *Homiletic Directory,* 54.

24. The Sunday came to be known as Quasimodo Sunday. In Victor Hugo's novel, *The Hunchback of Notre Dame,* the abandoned infant was said to have been found on this Sunday and given the name Quasimodo.

one of the two Entrance Antiphons given for this day in the Missal: "Like newborn infants, you must long for the pure, spiritual milk, that in him you may grow to salvation, alleluia."

We continually engage in mystagogy as we meditate on the Gospel, share in the Eucharist, and do charitable works.

We can glean two things from this. First, the neophytes need to make sense of all that happened to them at the Easter Vigil and in everything that led up to it. Having received the sacraments, they can understand their meanings more deeply than they could before. The homilies of Easter Time can certainly address some of this, but it is important to gather the neophytes a few times to reflect on the sacramental symbols. These sessions can be informal, more guided discussions than lectures. Prayer incorporating Scripture and the symbols of Easter should be part of such sessions. Videos and photos of the event may help call to mind each person's experience of the events. And food always encourages sharing.

The second thing we can glean is that the neophytes will be "newbies" for quite some time. They will still need support. While the formal time of mystagogy lasts for the fifty days until Pentecost, the bishops of the United States direct that

> After the immediate mystagogy or postbaptismal catechesis during the Easter season, the program for the neophytes should extend until the anniversary of Christian initiation, with at least monthly assemblies of the neophytes for their deeper Christian formation and incorporation into the full life of the Christian community.[25]

Like the immediate mystagogical gatherings, these can be informal times of prayer and conversation.

---

25. NS, 24.

"On the anniversary of their baptism the neophytes should be brought together in order to give thanks to God, to share with one another their spiritual experiences, and to renew their commitment."[26] The anniversary of the neophytes' initiation is the next year's Easter Vigil, even though it is not exactly the same date. They should certainly be encouraged to be there to rejoice with the newly baptized and to recall their initiation with a deeper understanding.

Many dioceses have a Mass for the neophytes with the bishop during Easter Time. If this is the case, the neophytes and their godparents should be encouraged to attend. If the bishop comes to the parish in the course of the year, try to arrange for him to meet the neophytes. If possible, have them sit together at a Mass at which the bishop presides.

In many ways, all of Christian life is mystagogical. We are always gaining deeper understanding of the Paschal Mystery through meditation on the Gospel, sharing in the Eucharist, and doing works of charity. This is the life of the Church until we come face to face with the Divine Mystery at our death.

---

26. RCIA, 250.

Preparing the Celebration of the Sacraments of Initiation outside the Easter Vigil

Those who are baptized are united to Christ in a death like his;
buried with him in death, they are given life again with him,
and with him they rise again.

Christian Initiation, General Introduction, 6

When Christian Initiation Occurs at a Different Time in the Liturgical Year

Only under extraordinary circumstances would the full initiation of an unbaptized person be celebrated outside the Easter Vigil. While the Vigil is certainly the premier time for initiation, the *Rite of Christian Initiation of Adults* states that there will be occasions when a person may be initiated at a time other than the Easter Vigil; such extraordinary circumstances might include delays because of military service or an extended postponement of initiation because of a long annulment process for an otherwise ready catechumen. It is important to note that any celebration of adult initiation outside the Easter Vigil requires the permission of the diocesan bishop.[1]

The Introduction to the *Rite of Christian Initiation of Adults* addresses the requirements for celebrating Christian initiation outside of the Easter Vigil.[2] Of particular note, paragraph 26 states, "When the time is changed . . . even though the rite of Christian initiation occurs at a different point in the liturgical year, the structure of the entire rite, with its properly spaced intervals, remains the same." This means that when a person is baptized outside the Easter Vigil, all the elements of the catechumenal process are still to be provided, particularly a Period of Purification and Enlightenment, even though that might not coincide with the season of Lent.

---

1. RCIA, 34 §2.
2. RCIA, 26–31.

Approximately six weeks, then, before the sacraments of initiation, the Rite of Election is to be celebrated. This could be celebrated by the diocesan bishop, or he could delegate a pastor to celebrate it in the parish of the catechumen. The Scrutinies would still be celebrated at their regular intervals during that six-week period of purification prior to the sacraments of initiation. Thus, approximately four weeks, then three weeks, then two weeks before the sacraments, the First, Second, and Third Scrutinies would be celebrated. These could be at the parish's Sunday Eucharist (as long as it was not a solemnity), and the Year A Scrutiny readings would be used. The Presentations of the Creed and of the Lord's Prayer would also be celebrated during this period of purification, prior to the sacraments of initiation

When initiation occurs outside the Easter Vigil, all the catechumenal elements are still provided.

The person would then be fully initiated at a Sunday celebration of Mass, according to the ritual of the RCIA, 218–243, and *The Roman Missal*. The Mass of the Sunday or the Mass For the Conferral of the Sacraments of Christian Initiation: 3. For the Conferral of Baptism would be used.

Celebrating Christian Initiation in Exceptional Circumstances

The situations surrounding initiation in exceptional circumstances can vary greatly, such as sickness, old age, change of residence, or long absence for travel.[3] A careful reading of the introductory material of Part II chapter 2, of the RCIA will help in determining the scope for adapting the celebration of initiation.

Some exceptional circumstances may require that the formation process cover a longer period of time; some rites may be combined as necessary, using the rite about to be described as a model.[4] Other exceptional circumstances may call for an abbreviated rite. In this celebration, the major rites

3. RCIA, 331–369.
4. RCIA, 332–335.

of the catechumenate are telescoped into a single rite[5] that resembles the *Rite of Baptism for Children.*

Receiving the Candidate: The celebration begins with Receiving the Candidate. This incorporates various elements and dynamics of the Rite of Acceptance into the Order of Catechumens. It begins either outside the church (if appropriate) or just inside the doors.

Greeting, Opening Dialogue, Candidate's Declaration, and Affirmation by the Godparents: The candidate, along with sponsors, family, friends, and some of the faithful, is greeted by the celebrant. He then asks the candidate, "What do you ask of the Church of God?" and the candidate declares his or her intention to receive the sacraments of initiation. The priest receives the affirmation of the godparents and then invites all to the celebration of the Word.

> Before the abbreviated form of the rite is celebrated the candidate must have gone through an adequate period of instruction and preparation before baptism, in order to purify his or her motives for requesting baptism and to grow stronger in conversion and faith.
>
> —*Rite of Christian Initiation of Adults*, 336

Intercessions for the Candidate: After the homily, the entire assembly offers intercessory prayer for the candidate, which is concluded by a Prayer of Exorcism over the candidate. Here, elements and dynamics of the Scrutiny rites are found. The Prayer of Exorcism is followed by the priest laying hands on the candidate's head and praying that Christ may strengthen him or her.

The text mentions an optional anointing with the Oil of Catechumens. However, the then National Conference of Catholic Bishops (now the United States Conference of Catholic Bishops) has decreed that this anointing is to take place during either the Period of the Catechumenate or the Period of Purification and Enlightenment, but not at the celebration of the sacraments of initiation.[6]

Celebration of Baptism: The celebration of Baptism begins with an introduction by the celebrant and a prayer over the waters; if the celebration takes place during the Easter season, then the Thanksgiving over Blessed Water is used. The candidate then renounces sin, professes the faith, and is baptized by the celebrant. The clothing with a baptismal garment and the

---

5. RCIA, 340–369.
6. RCIA, 352.

SECTION 1: PREPARING THE RITES FOR UNBAPTIZED ADULTS

presentation of a lighted candle follow. During this the assembly may sing an appropriate acclamation or song.

Celebration of Confirmation: The newly baptized is confirmed by the priest who performed the Baptism. The celebrant gives an introduction and then lays hands on the neophyte, followed by the prayer of Confirmation. The sponsor places the right hand on the shoulder of the candidate, who is confirmed with the usual formula.

The Universal Prayer follows and the newly baptized may assist in the Presentation of the Gifts. The celebration of the Eucharist includes the opportunity for the neophyte and others to receive the Eucharist under both kinds.

Initiation of a Person in Danger of Death

Part II, chapter 3,[7] of the *Rite of Christian Initiation of Adults* contains the rite to use when a person who is in danger of death is initiated. It is a shorter rite of initiation and is used primarily by catechists and other laypersons. If a priest or deacon is ministering to a person in danger of death, he would normally use the rite described previously, "In Exceptional Circumstances," except in case of an emergency.

Christian Initiation of a Person in Danger of Death is a brief rite, meant to respond to a critical situation. The Introductory Rites consist of questions posed to the person being baptized to establish his or her desire for Baptism and his or her intention to

> This shorter rite is designed particularly for use by catechists and laypersons; a priest or a deacon may use it in case of emergency.
>
> —*Rite of Christian Initiation of Adults*, 372

know Christ better should he or she recover health. The godparent(s) promise to help the candidate, should he or she recover, and all listen to a proclamation of Scripture.

Time and circumstances govern the Liturgy of the Word. The rite prescribes a brief proclamation and explanation of some portion from a Gospel. Five suggestions are given, but overall this is brief. Time may be of the essence.

The rite then provides intercessions for the candidate, if the situation warrants. This is quickly followed by the Rite of Baptism itself. There is the renunciation of sin and then the profession of faith. The person is baptized

---

7. RCIA, 370–399.

and, if the celebrant is a priest and chrism is available, Confirmation follows immediately.

—————————— ●●● ——————————

If persons who were baptized when in danger of death or at the point of death recover their health, they are to be given a suitable formation, be welcomed at the church in due time, and there receive the other sacraments of initiation.

—*Rite of Christian Initiation of Adults*, 374

Finally, the newly baptized and confirmed receives Viaticum, the final sharing in the Eucharist. This is reflected in the formulary from the minister that follows the giving of Communion: "May the Lord Jesus Christ protect you and lead you to eternal life."

Should the person recover his or her health, then he or she would continue formation as outlined for a baptized, uncatechized person.[8] In all of this, we see the Church's concern and care for one who has the desire for Baptism, and yet is faced with a serious crisis of health.

---

8. RCIA, 374.

SECTION 2

Preparing the Rites
for Baptized Adults

Preparing the Rites for Uncatechized Adults for Confirmation and Eucharist

Father of mercy,
we thank you for these servants.
You have already consecrated them in baptism
and now you call them
to the fullness of the Church's sacramental life:
we praise you, Lord, and we bless you.

—*Rite of Christian Initiation of Adults*, 420

P art I of the *Rite of Christian Initiation of Adults* deals with unbaptized individuals who seek initiation into Christ through the Sacraments of Baptism, Confirmation, and Eucharist. Part II considers people in particular circumstances related to receiving these sacraments. Chapter 4 of Part II is concerned with preparing people who were baptized either in the Roman Catholic Church or in another Christian community but who were never catechized.[1]

For a Roman Catholic, this presumes someone who never received Confirmation and Eucharist. Someone who received first Communion is presumed to have received some catechesis in the faith before receiving the sacrament. This process is not meant for catechized Catholics who missed receiving their Confirmation.

This process is also not meant for a baptized, practicing Christian of another faith community who wishes to be received into the full communion of the Catholic Church.

> As in the case of catechumens, the preparation of these adults requires a considerable time, during which the faith infused in baptism must grow in them and take deep root through the pastoral formation they receive.
>
> —*Rite of Christian Initiation of Adults*, 401

---

1. See RCIA, 400–472.

For uncatechized, baptized individuals of any denomination, a path of preparation similar to that of catechumens may be appropriate. They, like catechumens, need time to nurture faith, learn the teachings and traditions of the Church, and become familiar with the Christian community. These individuals are not catechumens.

Even though uncatechized adults have not yet heard the message of the mystery of Christ, their status differs from that of catechumens, since by baptism they have already become members of the Church and children of God. Hence their conversion is based on the baptism they have already received, the effects of which they must develop.[2]

> Just as it helps catechumens, the Christian community should also help these adults by its love and prayer and by testifying to their suitability when it is time for them to be admitted to the sacraments.
>
> —*Rite of Christian Initiation of Adults*, 403

An important aspect of the preparation of the baptized is the instillment of an appreciation and reverence for the Baptism they have already received. Their catechesis is postbaptismal; it consists in their coming to know and embrace, through Scripture and the Church, the Lord who has already claimed them as his children by adoption. They are already part of the Church by Baptism.

Once they have been welcomed into formation for the celebration of the Sacraments of Confirmation and Eucharist, they attend the Sunday Eucharist weekly.[3] Even though they are not yet sufficiently formed to receive the Body and Blood of Christ in Holy Communion, they can participate in the priestly actions of interceding for the world and praying the Eucharistic Prayer. For this reason, none of the Rites for Baptized but Uncatechized Adults includes a dismissal from the celebration of the Eucharist. Although some parishes dismiss baptized candidates at the same time as catechumens, a better approach may be to spend time early in the candidates' formation, separate from the catechumens, to help them understand how their Baptism has prepared them to participate in the prayer of the Church and how to do so until the time they can receive Holy Communion.

Unlike the catechumenate, the time of formation for baptized but uncatechized candidates does not necessarily culminate during Lent and the Easter

---

2. RCIA, 400.
3. RCIA, 413.

Vigil, although it certainly may. The baptized may participate in the catechesis and other activities prepared for the catechumens as appropriate. Although the baptized candidates are not yet participating in the Eucharist, they have already been initiated into Christ through Baptism.

The RCIA states, "The high point of their entire formation will normally be the Easter Vigil,"[4] but some parishes prefer to focus the Easter Vigil on the initiation of the elect alone. This does not necessarily mean delaying the celebration of Confirmation and Eucharist (and reception, if necessary) with the baptized until after Easter. If they are sufficiently prepared before Lent begins, they might receive the sacraments then so that they can fully par-

During their formation period, those who are uncatechized but baptized attend Sunday Eucharist weekly. They can participate in the priestly actions of interceding for the world and praying the Eucharistic Prayer.

ticipate in the Mass during the Lenten season. It may also be more ecumenically sensitive not to celebrate the reception of those baptized in other Christian traditions with all the ceremony that is afforded those being baptized. This is a pastoral issue that each parish should discuss.

Those baptized candidates who will be received into the full communion of the Catholic Church at the Vigil or at another time are confirmed by the priest who receives them at the same liturgy. He has this faculty by virtue of the law[5] and is required to exercise it.[6] Those candidates who are already baptized in the Catholic Church must be confirmed by the bishop, either at the Vigil or at another time, unless the presiding priest has been given delegation by the bishop to do so. Each diocese has its own regulations in this regard.

If sufficiently formed, baptized candidates may be received into the Church at any time during the year.

---

4. RCIA, 409.
5. CIC, c. 883 2°.
6. CIC, c. 885 §2.

Optional Rites for Baptized but Uncatechized Adults

The RCIA provides rites for the journey of the baptized, uncatechized candidates adapted from the rites for the unbaptized. These are optional rites, approved by the bishops of the United States; similar adaptations were approved by the bishops of Canada. The language of these rites makes it clear that these candidates are already baptized, and in some cases, changes in the ritual actions emphasize their difference from catechumens.

> In the process of catechesis the priest, deacon, or catechist should take into account that these adults have a special status because they are baptized.
>
> —*Rite of Christian Initiation of Adults,* 402

Combined rites for when catechumens and baptized candidates are present at the same time are addressed in the chapter "Preparing the Liturgies for the Combines Rites."[7]

Celebrating the Rite of Welcoming the Candidates

This optional rite usually takes place at a Sunday Eucharist, but may also take place at a Celebration of the Word of God. If this rite is to take place at a Sunday liturgy, a date should be chosen when the Scriptures of the day are appropriate for the purpose of the rite. If this rite is not celebrated, the candidates should be introduced to the community in another appropriate manner.

Since the baptized candidates have a place among the faithful, they are seated when the liturgy begins for the Rite of Welcoming the Candidates.

This rite is similar to the Rite of Acceptance into the Order of Catechumens, but it is simpler.[8] The liturgy begins in the usual way, with a procession of ministers. Because these candidates are baptized, they already have a place among the faithful,[9] where they are seated as the liturgy begins.

Welcoming the Candidates

Greeting: After the Entrance Procession, the celebrant greets the candidates

---

7. See pages 113–131.

8. See thechapter "Preparing the Rite of Acceptance into the Order of Catechumens," pages 21–39.

9. RCIA, 416.

and the whole assembly. He reminds the assembly that the new people among them are baptized. He then invites the candidates and their sponsors to come forward. If there is a large number, music may accompany this movement. The rite suggests Psalm 63:1–8.

Care should be taken to place the candidates in such a way that they can be seen by all in the assembly; if necessary, microphones should be provided so that all may hear their responses.

Opening Dialogue: The celebrant asks the candidates their name, and each replies; alternatively, the celebrant may call out the names of the candidates and have them reply "Present." He then asks them what they ask of the Church. They should be prepared to answer in their own words that they wish to be accepted for preparation leading to Confirmation and Eucharist or to reception into the full communion of the Catholic Church.

> The prayers and ritual gestures (of the Rite of Welcoming) acknowledge that such candidates are already part of the community because they have been marked by baptism.
>
> —*Rite of Christian Initiation of Adults,* 412

Candidates' Declaration of Intent and Affirmation by the Sponsors and the Assembly: The celebrant then asks the candidates to state their desire to continue the journey of faith, either in response to his question or in their own words.[10] He then asks the sponsors and assembly if they are ready to assist the candidates.

Signing of the Candidates with the Cross: The celebrant marks the candidates with the cross on their foreheads, with words that indicate that this is a reminder of their Baptism. The sponsors or catechist may also sign them. An acclamation may be sung, as at the Rite of Acceptance.

The celebrant may then sign the other senses, as at the Rite of Acceptance. In planning this liturgy, the initiation ministers and celebrant may wish to discuss whether the multiple signing is too similar to the prebaptismal signing at the Rite of Acceptance.[11]

---

10. See RCIA, 419.
11. The Canadian version of this rite includes only the signing of the forehead.

Liturgy of the Word

After a brief instruction to the candidates, the Word is proclaimed in the usual way and the homily is preached on the Scriptures, taking into account the presence of those beginning their preparations.

Presentation of a Bible: After the homily, candidates may be called forward so that the celebrant may present them a Bible (or a book containing the Gospels). This may be a Bible that is given for each to keep, or it may be a large Bible or the *Book of the Gospels* used at Mass that is presented in a ritual manner and then reverenced by each candidate in turn. An acclamation could accompany this action. This rite is optional.

During the Rite of Welcoming, the celebrant signs the cross on the candidate's forehead, using words that recall their Baptism.

Profession of Faith: The Creed is recited on Sundays and solemnities.

Universal Prayer and Prayer over the Candidates: Intercessions for the candidates are included in the Universal Prayer, which concludes with a prayer prayed by the celebrant with hands outstretched over the candidates.

Dismissal of the Assembly or Liturgy of the Eucharist: If the Eucharist is not celebrated, all are dismissed. If the Liturgy of the Eucharist is celebrated, it begins as usual with the Preparation of the Altar and the Gifts. The candidates are not dismissed, nor do they present the gifts.

Rite of Sending the Candidates for Recognition by the Bishop and the Call to Continuing Conversion

This Rite of Sending[12] may be celebrated when the candidates will be sent to the celebration of the Rite of Calling the Candidates to Continuing Conversion. The Rite of Sending is celebrated prior to the Rite of Calling, usually at a Sunday Eucharist, or at a Celebration of the Word. It is similar to the optional Rite of Sending Catechumens for Election, but simpler; see notes on that rite on pages 56–58. The rite does not call for the signing of the Book of the Elect by the candidates; parishes should follow the practice of their diocese. Notes for the combined rite when candidates and catechumens are sent to the bishop are found on 122–125.

---

12. RCIA, 434–445.

Presentation of the Candidates: After the homily, the minister in charge of the formation of candidates presents them to the celebrant for recognition of the progress they have made and the assurance of the community's prayers. The candidates are called forward by name and go with their sponsors to the celebrant. They should stand so the assembly may see their faces.

Affirmation by the Sponsors and the Assembly: The celebrant asks the sponsors and assembly to affirm the readiness of the candidates.

Universal Prayer and Prayer over the Candidates: Intentions for the candidates are prayed, which concludes with a prayer by the celebrant, prayed with hands outstretched over the candidates. If this rite takes place at a celebration of the Eucharist, the usual intercessions for the Church and the world may be included.

Dismissal of the Assembly or Liturgy of the Eucharist: If the Eucharist is not celebrated, all are dismissed. If the Liturgy of the Eucharist is celebrated, it begins as usual with the Preparation of Altar and the Gifts. The candidates are not dismissed, nor do they present the gifts. For pastoral reasons, the Profession of Faith may be omitted.[13]

Penitential Rite (Scrutiny)

The RCIA offers the option of celebrating the Penitential Rite for the baptized candidates.[14] It is designed to be celebrated on the Second Sunday of Lent, but it may be celebrated on a Lenten weekday or at another suitable time. If the Penitential Rite is celebrated on the Second Sunday of Lent, the Mass and the readings are from that day; if it is celebrated on another day, appropriate readings from the Lectionary are used,[15] and the Collect provided in the rite is prayed.[16] This rite follows a pattern similar to the Scrutinies; instead of focusing on preparation for Baptism, however, the texts and prayers look to preparation for Reconciliation. The candidates will receive the Sacrament of Reconciliation before they are confirmed, share in the Eucharist and, if appropriate, are received into the full Communion of the Catholic Church.

Suggestions for celebrating the Scrutinies may help in preparing this rite; those suggestions are found on pages 59–63. There is no ritual Mass for the Penitential Rite as there are for the Scrutinies. There is no combined rite

---

13. RCIA, 445.
14. RCIA, 459–472.
15. RCIA, 466.
16. RCIA, 465.

for the Scrutinies and the Penitential Rite. The prayers and other texts of the Scrutinies are specific to the elect; they include prebaptismal exorcisms, which are not appropriate to the baptized.

Celebrating the Penitential Rite (Scrutiny)

Introductory Rites: During the Introductory Rites, the celebrant "explains that the rite will have different meanings for the different participants . . . particularly those who are preparing to celebrate the sacrament of penance for the first time. . . . All . . . are going to hear the comforting message of pardon for sin, for which they will praise the Father's mercy."[17]

Invitation to Silent Prayer: After the homily, the candidates are called forward with their sponsors. After instructions to the assembly and the candidates to pray in silence, the priest invites the candidates to bow their heads or to kneel. The sponsors remain standing; the assembly remains seated. The entire community prays silently for the candidates; after a substantial period of silence, all stand for the intercessions.

> Because the penitential rite normally belongs to the period of final preparation for the sacraments, its celebration presumes that the candidates are approaching the maturity of faith and understanding requisite for fuller life in the community.
>
> —*Rite of Christian Initiation of Adults*, 460

Universal Prayer and Prayer over the Candidates: Intentions for the candidates are prayed; if this rite takes place at a celebration of the Eucharist, the usual intercessions for the Church and the world may be included. After the intercessions, the celebrant prays aloud, with hands outstretched over the candidates. Two Prayers over the Candidates are provided; option A is most appropriate on the Second Sunday of Lent.

Dismissal of the Assembly or Liturgy of the Eucharist: If the Eucharist is not celebrated, all are dismissed. If the Liturgy of the Eucharist is celebrated, it begins as usual with the Preparation of the Altar and the Gifts. The candidates are not dismissed, nor do they present the gifts. For pastoral reasons, the Profession of Faith may be omitted.[18]

---

17. RCIA, 464.
18. RCIA, 472.

Preparing the Rite for the Reception of Baptized Christians into the Full Communion of the Catholic Church

The rite is so arranged that no greater burden than necessary (see Acts 15:28) is required for the establishment of communion and unity.

—Rite of Christian Initiation of Adults, 473

The Rite of Reception of Baptized Christians into the Full Communion of the Catholic Church[1] originally existed apart from the *Rite of Christian Initiation of Adults* in the Church's liturgical corpus. When the Church reestablished the catechumenal process of initiation, this rite was included in the RCIA to address the needs of the baptized who sought unity with the Catholic Church.

The purpose of this rite is to establish communion and unity with those who are baptized in a separated ecclesial community and who seek to be received into the fullness of communion. People who have been baptized in another Christian community may or may not need an extended period of catechesis in preparation for reception. Those who do are prepared according to the process indicated in the "Preparation of Uncatechized Adults for Confirmation and Eucharist"[2] and *National Statutes,* 32. Many who wish to be received are catechized and practicing Christians; some have already been participating in Catholic worship for a period of time. These individuals should have the opportunity to learn the teachings and traditions particular to the

> Those who have already been baptized in another Church or ecclesial community should not be treated as catechumens or so designated.
>
> *—National Statutes for the Catechumenate,* 30

---

1. RCIA, 473–504.
2. RCIA, 400–472.

Catholic Church, but an extensive catechesis is usually not needed. For the sake of communion and unity "no greater burden than necessary (see Acts 15:28) is required."[3] A sponsor should accompany each candidate through the process of formation.

For those baptized persons who are seeking full communion, there is no specified time for reception, as there is for the unbaptized. While many parishes receive baptized Christians at the Easter Vigil, the reception may take place at other times. In fact, the *National Statutes for the Catechumenate* state that "it is preferable that reception into full communion not take place at the Easter Vigil."[4]

———————————————●●—————————————

> The celebration of the sacrament of reconciliation with candidates for reception into full communion is to be carried out at a time prior to and distinct from the celebration of the rite of reception.
>
> —*National Statutes for the Catechumenate*, 36

Rather, the reception of baptized Christians may take place at any time during the year, "at the Sunday Eucharist of the parish community."[5] In other words, baptized Christians are received into full communion, when they are ready. As candidates are discerned to be ready for reception, a Sunday in the near future when the readings of the Mass seem appropriate might be chosen. While the Rite of Reception may be celebrated outside Mass, it makes the most sense to celebrate the rite within Mass, since the culmination of communion and unity would in fact be the sharing in the Eucharist.

Prior to celebrating this rite, candidates should celebrate the Sacrament of Reconciliation. Any priest who has the faculty to absolve sins can celebrate this with them.[6]

Celebrating the Rite of Reception

If reception is celebrated on a Sunday or solemnity, the readings of the day are used. If it is celebrated on another day, readings may be taken from the

---

3. RCIA, 473.

4. NS, 33. This seems to conflict with RCIA, 409, located in the chapter "Preparation of Uncatechized Adults for Confirmation and Eucharist": "The high point of their entire formation will normally be the Easter Vigil. At that time they will make a profession of the faith in which they were baptized, receive the sacrament of confirmation, and take part in the Eucharist." It should be noted, however, that this section was originally intended for baptized, uncatechized Catholics.

5. NS, 32.

6. NS, 36.

day, or from the celebration of reception into full communion, or from the Mass "For Christian Unity." If the Mass is not celebrated at an ordinarily scheduled Sunday Mass, the parish should be invited to participate in the liturgy, and a full complement of liturgical ministries—including greeters, music ministers, and trained readers—should serve.

Invitation

After the homily, the celebrant invites the candidate and sponsor forward. While a text is provided in the rite, the celebrant may also use his own words,[7] which will allow for a certain personalization of the celebration.

> It is preferable that reception into full communion not take place at the Easter Vigil lest there be any confusion of such baptized Christians with the candidates for baptism, possible misunderstanding of or even reflection upon the sacrament of baptism celebrated in another Church or ecclesial community, or any perceived triumphalism in the liturgical welcome into the Catholic eucharistic community.
>
> —*National Statutes for the Catechumenate*, 33

Profession of Faith

With the whole liturgical assembly, the candidate recites the Nicene Creed. After the Creed, the candidate alone adds, "I believe and profess all that the holy Catholic Church believes, teaches, and proclaims to be revealed by God."[8]

Act of Reception

The celebrant proclaims that "the Lord receives you into the Catholic Church." If Confirmation is not taking place at this liturgy, he lays hands on the candidate's head as he says this.

Confirmation

The celebrant lays hands on the head of the candidate, then prays the prayer

While the celebrant anoints the candidate on the forehead, the sponsor's right hand is on the candidate's shoulder.

of Confirmation. As the sponsor places the right hand on the shoulder of the candidate, the celebrant anoints the candidate on the forehead while saying

---

7. RCIA, 490.
8. RCIA, 491.

the formula for Confirmation. The celebrant then offers the newly confirmed the sign of peace.[9]

Celebrant's Sign of Welcome

Whether Confirmation is celebrated or not, the celebrant offers a sign of welcome, friendship, and acceptance. In many parishes the entire assembly offers applause, or may even sing a joyful antiphon. Parishes need to take care, though, that the joy of this reception would not be perceived as triumphalism.

Universal Prayer

The Universal Prayer includes intercessions for the newly received and for the unity of the Church.

Sign of Peace

After the Universal Prayer, the rite allows for a sign of peace in which the entire assembly greets the newly received. However, since most parishes celebrate the rite of reception at Sunday Mass, the sign of peace would seem best done at its usual place.

The newly received taking part in Communion for the first time is the culmination of reception and union with the Church.

Liturgy of the Eucharist

Mass continues with the Liturgy of the Eucharist. The newly received and others may present the gifts of bread and wine. The culmination of reception into the full communion of the Catholic Church is when the newly received take part in Holy Communion for the first time. The newly received and his or her sponsor may receive the Eucharist under both kinds, even if this is not the usual practice of the parish.

Preparing the Liturgies of the Combined Rites

> In the catechesis of the community and in the celebration of these rites,
> care must be taken to maintain the distinction between the catechumens
> and the baptized candidates.
>
> —*Rite of Christian Initiation of Adults*, 506

The Combined Rites are found in appendix I of the RCIA, titled "Additional (Combined) Rites." They were crafted in response to the pastoral situation in the United States, where many parishes often have as many or more baptized candidates than catechumens. Combining the two categories of people into one celebration is one response. Celebrating the rites for the unbaptized and the baptized at different times is another. However the rites are celebrated, it is imperative that the distinction between the baptized and the unbaptized is made and is clear to the assembly, by word and action. Baptism makes a difference.

These combined rites are all constructed similarly. At most points in the rite, the unbaptized are addressed first, then the baptized. To make these two groups more evident, they should be placed apart from each other so that it is clear that two related but essentially different things are occurring.

In the catechesis of the community and in the celebration of these rites, care must be taken to maintain the distinction between the catechumens and the baptized candidates.

—*Rite of Christian Initiation of Adults*, 506

Celebrating the Combined Rites of Acceptance and Welcoming

This rite is similar to the Rite of Acceptance into the Order of Catechumens.[1] It may be helpful to look at the chapter "Preparing the Rite of Acceptance into the Order of Catechumens for the notes on preparing that rite. This rite

---

1. See pages 21–39.

usually takes place at a Sunday Mass or a Celebration of the Word. As with the Rite of Acceptance, this rite serves as the Entrance Rite of the Mass or Celebration of the Word at which it takes place.

The structure of the rite is as follows:

Receiving the Candidates

- Greeting
- Opening Dialogue with Candidates for the Catechumenate and with the Candidates for Post-baptismal Catechesis
- Catechumens' First Acceptance of the Gospel
- Candidates' Declaration of Intent
- Affirmation by the Sponsors and the Assembly
- Signing of the Catechumens and the Candidates with the Sign of the Cross
  - Signing of the Forehead of the Catechumens
  - Signing of the Other Senses (optional)
  - Signing of the Forehead of the Candidates
  - Signing of the Other Senses of the Candidates (optional)
- Concluding Prayer
- Invitation to the Celebration of the Word of God

Liturgy of the Word

- Instruction
- Readings
- Homily
- Presentation of a Bible (optional)
- Intercessions for the Catechumens and Candidates
- Prayer over the Catechumens and Candidates
- Dismissal of the Catechumens

The rite begins when the inquirers and the baptized candidates, who have gathered at the appointed place outside the church (or inside the doors of the church) with their sponsors and other members of the faithful[2] are greeted by the celebrant. If the assembly consists of more than those who are

---

2. RCIA, 507.

gathered with the inquirers and candidates, the celebrant could begin in the church and invite those inside to accompany him for the greeting; if the rite will take place at the back of the church, the celebrant or another minister may invite the assembly to turn to the back of the church. As he walks toward the inquirers, a psalm or appropriate song may be sung.

Although the rite does not mention it, the celebrant could appropriately be accompanied by ministers carrying a processional cross and candles. The presence of the cross is a powerful sign as the inquirers and candidates commit themselves to walk in Christ's way.

Afterward, depending on the placement of the celebrant in relation to the inquirers, the inquirers may move forward to stand in front of the celebrant accompanied by song; Psalm 63:1–8 is suggested. In practice, this is rarely done.

Receiving the Candidates

Greeting: The celebrant's greeting to the inquirers and candidates is meant to be informal and personal, expressing the Church's joy at their presence and perhaps discreetly sharing a bit of their spiritual journey to this point.

At this very beginning point, the celebrant should make clear that those being welcomed are of two categories: the unbaptized and the baptized.

Opening Dialogue with Candidates for the Catechumenate and with the Candidates for Post-baptismal Catechesis: The celebrant then introduces the candidates to the assembly by asking each their name or by calling their names,

As the celebrant dialogues with the unbaptized and baptized individuals, he adapts the questions to the status of those being welcomed.

unbaptized first. The celebrant then asks the candidates individually about their intentions in coming to the Church, unbaptized first. The celebrant has great flexibility in how this takes place,[3] but he should adapt the questions to the differing status of those being welcomed. The candidates should know

---

3. RCIA, 509.

that these questions will be asked; it may be helpful for their catechists or sponsors to help them consider their answers beforehand.

Catechumens' First Acceptance of the Gospel: The celebrant then invites the unbaptized to express their willingness to follow the way of Christ found in the Gospel. The rite suggests that the celebrant adapt this invitation to be responsive to what the inquirers and candidates have expressed in answering the previous questions. The inquirers should be prepared to respond, "I am."

On very rare occasions, it may be appropriate to replace the first acceptance of the Gospel with an exorcism and renunciation of false worship. This is to be done only with the permission of the diocesan bishop and is primarily to be used in "regions where false worship is widespread" where one may have engaged in occult practices, such as "worshiping spiritual powers . . . calling on the shades of the dead or . . . using magical arts."[4] It is not meant as a repudiation of other established religions the inquirer may have adhered to.

Candidates' Declaration of Intent: The celebrant then asks the candidates to state their desire to continue the journey of faith.[5]

Affirmation by the Sponsors and the Assembly: The celebrant asks the sponsors and assembly if they are ready to assist the candidates. They answer in the affirmative. A prayer of praise follows, to which the assembly is to respond in speech or song.[6] Unless the response, which is the same as the last line of the prayer, is given in the worship aid, it might help for the cantor or another minister to sing or proclaim the response and then gesture for all to repeat it.

If the cantor sings the response after the sponsors affirm the inquirers' readiness, and then gestures to the faithful, all will be encouraged to participate.

Signing of the Forehead (and other Senses) of the Catechumens: Those who are becoming catechumens are signed as a group before the baptized candidates are signed. If the place where all have gathered does not allow everyone to see the signings, many parishes move into the church at this point, especially if

---

4. RCIA, 70.
5. RCIA, 512.
6. RCIA, 513.

the signing of the senses will be included. Psalm 63:1–8, or a reprise of what was sung as the celebrant approached the inquirers might appropriately accompany this movement.

The rite envisions that the signing will take place where the earlier parts of the ritual have taken place, so do so if it is possible. This will help emphasize the symbolism of the catechumens' entrance into the church to hear the Word of God at the end of the rite.

The celebrant invites the catechumens and their sponsors forward for the signing.[7] If everyone has just entered the church from outside, wait until all are seated and settled. In that case, it may also be better for the catechumens, baptized candidates, and sponsors to wait in the back of the church until they are called forward.

When preparing this liturgy, consider where the catechumens and sponsors will stand for their signings. The signing is a powerful symbol not only for the individual, but for the whole assembly as well. Depending on the size and configuration of the church, the catechumens may be placed across the front of the church, facing the assembly; they might also be placed in the aisles, some near the front of the church, some closer to the back, so that all the members of the assembly can see this important action.

The celebrant speaks the formula as the sponsor signs the senses.

If there are only a few catechumens, the celebrant signs the forehead of each, repeating the given formula for each; if they are placed around the church, he may go to each one. Each sponsor then signs their inquirer as well, if there will be no further signings. If there are many inquirers, they take their places with their sponsors. The celebrant says a few words of explanation, then makes the Sign of the Cross over them all while saying the formula. At the same time, the sponsor or catechist signs them on the forehead.[8]

If the senses are also to be signed,[9] the celebrant speaks the formula for each sense as the sponsor or catechist does the signing. The acclamation is

---

7. RCIA, 515.
8. RCIA, 515.
9. RCIA, 516.

sung after each signing. The signing concludes with the celebrant making the Sign of the Cross over the candidates, individually or all at once, while saying, "I sign you with the sign of eternal life in the name of the Father, and of the Son, and of the Holy Spirit"; the new catechumens reply, "Amen." A concluding prayer is prayed.

An acclamation is sung after each signing; the rite suggests "Glory and praise to you, Lord Jesus Christ," for which most parishes will already have a musical setting, since it is one of the Lenten Gospel acclamations. Another appropriate acclamation may be sung.

The text for the signing of the candidates recalls their Baptism.

Signing of the Forehead (and Other Senses) of the Candidates: The candidates are then called forward to be signed, and they take their places. The text for the celebrant as he performs the first signing is adapted to reflect that this signing recalls their Baptism, by which they have been claimed by Christ. It may serve to differentiate further the difference between the baptized and the unbaptized if only the signing of the forehead recalling their Baptism is performed. Otherwise, the signing of the senses is performed in the same way as for the catechumens.

Concluding Prayer and Invitation to the Celebration of the Word of God: The concluding prayer is prayed and all take their seats in the church.

Liturgy of the Word

After a brief instruction by the celebrant regarding the dignity of the Word of God, the readings are proclaimed. They may be those of the day or, if permitted, other readings may be chosen.[10] The homily is preached on the readings.

Presentation of a Bible: After the homily, the catechumens and the baptized candidates may be called forward so that a Bible (or a book containing the Gospels) may be presented to them by the celebrant. This may be a Bible that is given for each catechumen to keep, or it may be a large Bible or the *Book of the Gospels* used at Mass that is presented in a ritual manner and

---

10. RCIA, 523, provides suggestions.

then reverenced by each person in turn. A cross may also be given. An acclamation could accompany this action. This rite is optional.[11]

Intercessions for the Catechumens and Candidates: The assembly then prays for the catechumens and candidates. They may be invited to stand facing the assembly, if they are not already in that position, as the assembly prays. These are prayers of intercession similar in structure to the Universal Prayer, but specific in nature. A response different from that customarily used at Mass may emphasize the difference. Because intercessory prayer is the duty of the baptized, the catechumens are silent during this prayer.

If the rite is being celebrated at Mass, the Universal Prayer may be prayed after the catechumens are dismissed, or it may be omitted. In that case, intentions for the Church and the world are added to the intercessions for the catechumens.[12]

Prayer over the Catechumens and Candidates: A prayer spoken by the celebrant with hands outstretched over the catechumens and candidates concludes the intercessions and the Rite of Acceptance.[13]

During the intercessions, the assembly prays for the catechumens and candidates.

Dismissal: If the Rite of Acceptance and Welcoming has been celebrated outside Mass, everyone is dismissed at this point.[14]

If the Liturgy of the Eucharist is to follow, the catechumens, but not the baptized candidates, are normally dismissed to continue reflecting on the Word of God. The catechumens and their catechist may be invited forward before the words of dismissal are spoken. They should have their coats, purses, and other belongings with them. The celebrant expresses the great joy of the rite just celebrated and dismisses the catechumens with words of peace. Two suggested formulas are given.[15] Music, preferably a refrain sung by the whole assembly, may accompany the procession. The sponsors and candidates remain until the end of Mass and may join the catechumens at that time.

---

11. RCIA, 525.
12. RCIA, 529.
13. RCIA, 527.
14. RCIA, 528D.
15. RCIA 528A, B.

Should there be a reason that the catechumens cannot be dismissed, they are invited to remain and gently reminded that they must await the day of their Baptism before they may participate fully at the Lord's table. A sample formula for this situation is provided.[16] Catechumens are never dismissed simply to go home at this point.

Liturgy of the Eucharist

When the Liturgy of the Eucharist follows, the Universal Prayer may be prayed. It could be introduced as a continuation of the Intercessions for the Catechumens and Candidates (for example, "Let us continue to pray for the needs of the Church and the world") or it could be introduced in the usual way. As mentioned previously, the Universal Prayer may be omitted. In addition, the Profession of Faith may be omitted[17] and the liturgy continue with the Preparation of the Altar and the Gifts (the candidates do not bring forward the gifts). These permissions recognize that this rite may take a bit more time than the ordinary Introductory Rites and allow the rite to be celebrated in an unhurried manner.

Parish Celebration for Sending Catechumens for Election and Candidates for Recognition by the Bishop

The Rite of Sending the Catechumens for Election and Candidates for Recognition by the Bishop is an optional rite, and it is particular to the Church in the United States. This rite closely resembles the Rite of Sending for Election; the notes for preparing and celebrating the Rite of Sending in the chapter "Preparing Rites Belonging to the Period of the Catechumenate" may be useful in preparing this rite.[18]

Normally, this combined rite takes place near the First Sunday of Lent, before the catechumens and candidates go to the cathedral for the celebration of the rites of Election and the Call to Continuing Conversion.

Discernment is presumed to have taken place since, as the rite states, "the Church judges their [the catechumens'] state of readiness and decides on their advancement toward the sacraments of initiation. Thus the Church makes its 'election,' that is, the choice and admission of those catechumens

---

16. RCIA, 528C.
17. RCIA, 529.
18. See pages 53–57.

SECTION 2: PREPARING THE RITES FOR BAPTIZED ADULTS

who have the dispositions that make them fit to take part, at the next major celebration, in the sacraments of initiation."[19] A similar discernment for the readiness of the baptized to receive the Sacraments of Confirmation and Eucharist, and for reception, if appropriate, is also to be made.

As with all the combined rites, the distinction between the catechumens and candidates is to be maintained. Note that the rite states that only the catechumens sign the Book of the Elect. The election of the candidates for Baptism has already been demonstrated by the fact that they are baptized. The parish should follow the practice of the diocese.

Presentation of the Catechumens: After the homily, an appropriate minister, such as the coordinator of initiation ministry, first presents the catechumens to be sent for election to the celebrant. The rite provides a formula with which to present them, noting that the catechumens have progressed in their formation and conver-

Only the catechumens sign the Book of the Elect at the Rite for Sending Catechumens for Election and Candidates for Recognition by the Bishop.

sion and attesting that they are ready to be sent to the cathedral. This presentation may be adapted and personalized according to the specific circumstances of the catechumens.

The celebrant then calls the catechumens by name to come forward with those who will be their godparents. They come forward to stand before the celebrant.

Affirmation by the Godparents [and the Assembly]: The celebrant first addresses the people, reminding them of their responsibility in assessing the readiness of the catechumens. He then turns to the godparents, who to some degree represent the rest of the people of the parish, and asks for their testimony as to the readiness of the catechumens. He asks whether the catechumens have "taken their formation in the Gospel and in the Catholic way of life seriously," whether they have "given evidence of their conversion by the example of their lives," and whether the godparents judge them "to be ready to be presented to the bishop for the rite of election."[20] To each of these questions, the godparents are expected to answer in the affirmative.

---

19. RCIA, 119.
20. RCIA, 538.

The celebrant may turn back to the people and ask for their approval of the catechumens. This can be a very powerful way for the people of the parish to claim their responsibility in the progress of formation and conversion of the catechumens. It reminds us that "the people of God, as represented by the local Church, should understand and show by their concern that the initiation of adults is the responsibility of all the baptized."[21]

This might be done by the celebrant asking, "People of St. N. Parish, I now ask you: Do you judge these catechumens, with whom you have walked during their formation and conversion, to be ready to be presented to the bishop for election?" The people would then respond, "We do."

The celebrant may ask the assembly for their approval of the candidates.

The celebrant then turns back to the catechumens and declares that the parish community has judged them ready and recommends them to the bishop to be elected in the name of Christ.

The Book of the Elect may be signed at this point, unless it is to be signed at the diocesan celebration. Note that the rite states that only the catechumens sign the Book of the Elect. The election of the candidates for Baptism has already been demonstrated by the fact that they are baptized. The parish should follow the practice of the diocese.

Presentation of the Candidates: A minister then presents the candidates to be sent for recognition by the bishop. The rite also provides a formula for this presentation.[22] The celebrant then calls the candidates by name to come forward with their sponsors. They come forward to stand before the celebrant.

The celebrant first addresses the people, referring to the candidates as "already one with us by reason of their Baptism in Christ." He turns to the sponsors and asks for their testimony as to the readiness of the candidates. He may also turn back to the people for their approval.

---

21. RCIA, 9.
22. RCIA, 540.

The celebrant then turns to the candidates and declares that the parish community accepts the testimony of their sponsors and sends them to the bishop "who will exhort you to live in deeper conformity to the life of Christ."[23]

Intercessions for the Catechumens and Candidates and Prayer over the Catechumens and Candidates: The whole assembly then prays for the catechumens and candidates in the intercessions. Although the rite provides texts that can be used in the intercessions, it also notes that these texts may be personalized or otherwise adapted to fit various circumstances. The intercessions conclude with the Prayer over the Catechumens, which the presider prays with hands outstretched over the catechumens.

Dismissal: If the Eucharist is to follow, the catechumens, but not the candidates, are dismissed in the usual manner. If not, all are dismissed.

Liturgy of the Eucharist: If the Eucharist is to follow, the usual intercessions in the Universal Prayer may follow, or they may be omitted, in which case, the intercessions for the Church and the world would have been included in the intercessions for the catechumens. The Mass continues with the Creed, although for pastoral reasons, it too may be omitted. The Preparation of the Altar and the Gifts follows as usual.[24]

Celebration at the Easter Vigil of the Sacraments of Initiation and of the Rite of Reception into the Full Communion of the Catholic Church

> Pastoral considerations may suggest that along with the celebration of the sacraments of Christian initiation the Easter Vigil should include the rite of reception of already baptized Christians into the full communion of the Catholic Church. But such a decision must be guided by the theological and pastoral directives proper to each rite.[25]

Ecumenical issues should be taken into consideration in making the decision to receive candidates during the Easter Vigil. The candidates should be consulted in making this decision; "local conditions and . . . personal and family preferences" should also be considered.[26]

Consideration of the balance between the number of people to be baptized and the number to be received might also be included in the

---

23. RCIA, 542.
24. RCIA, 117.
25. RCIA, 562.
26. RCIA, 564.

decision-making process. Consistently celebrating the Vigil with a small number of elect and many candidates to be received may overshadow the centrality of Baptism into the Paschal Mystery of Christ.

Additionally, if a bishop will be present or if the celebrant has received delegation from the diocesan bishop to confirm baptized Catholics, those Catholic candidates who have undergone a process of catechesis in preparation for the Sacraments of Confirmation and Eucharist[27] will be confirmed.

In any case, care must be taken to indicate that the "candidates have already been incorporated into Christ in baptism and anything that would equate them with catechumens is to be absolutely avoided."[28]

Notes for preparing for the celebration of the sacraments of initiation may be found in the chapter "Preparing the Celebration of the Sacraments of Initiation at the Easter Vigil."[29]

The liturgy has the following structure:

Service of Light

Liturgy of the Word

Celebration of Baptism

- Presentation of the Candidates for Baptism

- Invitation to Prayer

- Litany of the Saints

- Blessing of the Water

- Profession of Faith

  ◻ Renunciation of Sin

  ◻ Profession of Faith

- Baptism

- Explanatory Rites

  ◻ Clothing with a Baptismal Garment (optional)

  ◻ Presentation of a Lighted Candle

---

27. RCIA, 409.
28. RCIA, 565.
29. See pages 78–98.

Renewal of Baptismal Promises

- Invitation
- Renewal of Baptismal Promises
  - Renunciation of Sin
  - Profession of Faith
- Sprinkling with Baptismal Water

Celebration of Reception

- Invitation
- Profession by Candidates
- Act of Reception

Celebration of Confirmation

- Laying on of Hands
- Anointing of Chrism

Celebrating the Sacraments of Initiation at the Easter Vigil

Service of Light

The Church, including the elect and the candidates, gathers at the fire. Position the elect near the fire, wearing their prebaptismal robes, if they are used, so they can fully experience this powerful sign and so that they can be signs of new life to the rest of the assembly. Let the elect and the candidates follow immediately behind the Paschal candle as it leads the assembly into the dark church. By being immediately behind the Paschal candle, they can more easily take their reserved seats as the faithful process in behind them.

Liturgy of the Word

For the Paschal Vigil, the Lectionary presents nine readings, seven from the Old Testament and two from the New Testament. For pastoral reasons fewer Old Testament readings may be used, however, note that the Exodus reading must always be used. Consider using all the readings, especially when there are elect to be baptized.

These stories tell of God's powerful acts of salvation throughout history. This night, the elect are added to this story. They are the next chapter in this great history of God's saving presence and action in the world, in our midst.

Celebration of Baptism

Presentation of the Elect and the Litany of the Saints: There are three options for the presentation of the candidates, depending upon the layout of each parish church and upon how the Baptisms will take place.[30]

If there is to be no procession to the font, option A is used. The celebrant goes immediately to the font after the homily and the elect are called forward, together with their godparents. In this case, the invitation to prayer and the Litany of the Saints follow while all stand in their place.

If there is to be a procession to the font, option B is used. It calls for the elect to process behind the deacon or other minister carrying the Paschal candle to the font. The celebrant follows the elect and godparents. During the procession, the Litany of the Saints is sung. This option suits well those churches that have a substantial font with its own space somewhere in the church.

In deciding which option to use, consider the liturgical symbolism of a procession. It is a way of praying with our bodies, a physical enactment of our prayer. It symbolizes the great pilgrimage we make to the heavenly Jerusalem, the journey of faith that we make throughout our lives, including the journey that the elect have been making in the process of their conversion.

If option B is used, once the procession reaches the font, the celebrant gives the invitation to prayer and the blessing of the water takes place immediately.

When the catechumens have assembled close to the font, the celebrant blesses the baptismal water.

If the parish does not have a substantial font with its own space within the church, or if the font is a fixed font located in the sanctuary, option C, when Baptism is celebrated in the sanctuary, can be used. A minister calls the elect forward, together with their godparents, and the invitation to prayer is given, followed by the singing of the Litany of the Saints.

Both options A and C allow for the Litany of the Saints to be sung after all the elect have been called by name, and while all of them make their way to the font. All three options call for the positioning of the candidates at the font in such a way that the full congregation might witness the Baptisms.

---

30. RCIA, 219.

Blessing of the Water: Once all have assembled around the baptismal font, the celebrant prays the Prayer over the Water.

Profession of Faith: There are two parts to the Profession of Faith: the renunciation of sin and the profession of faith. "The elect . . . renounce sin and Satan in order to commit themselves for ever to the promise of the Savior and to the mystery of the Trinity."[31] It is important that everyone in the church is able to hear the elect make this renunciation and profession. In their preparation, the elect might be guided in responding strongly; if needed, microphones could be used.

Either the translation in *The Roman Missal* or that found in the *Rite of Christian Initiation of Adults* may be used.[32]

The elect may make the renunciation as a group or individually.[33] The Profession of Faith is done individually, unless there are "a great many" to be baptized, when the profession may be done in a group. Each of the elect is baptized immediately after making his or her profession.[34]

With a godparent touching the shoulder of the elect, the priest pours water three times.

Baptism: Each of the elect comes to the font for Baptism individually. If the method is by immersion, the elect steps into the font. With one or both godparents touching the elect, the priest immerses the elect three times under the water using the customary formulary: "N., I baptize you in the name of the Father," as he immerses the first time; "and of the Son," as he immerses a second time, "and of the Holy Spirit" as he immerses a third time. If the method of Baptism is to pour water over the whole body of the elect (which is still a form of immersion), the elect stands or kneels in the font as the priest says, "N., I baptize you in the name of the Father," as he pours water over the full body a first time, "and of the Son," as he pours water a second time, "and of the Holy Spirit" as he pours water over the full body a third time.

---

31. RCIA, 211.

32. Letter dated November 30, 2011, by Archbishop Gregory M. Aymond, chairman of the Bishops' Committee on Divine Worship.

33. RCIA, 224.

34. RCIA, 225.

If Baptism is by means of infusion, where the elect approaches the font and leans his or her head over it, then one or both godparents place the right hand on the shoulder of the elect. The celebrant pours water over the forehead three times, saying the formulary as the water is poured.

No matter how the Baptisms are conferred, remember that Christ Jesus stands before us this night, alive in his new members. This is a moment of great joy for the parish community and indeed for the whole Church.

Explanatory Rites: The Explanatory Rites give expression to what has just been celebrated, to what God has just done in our midst.[35] These rites consist of the anointing after Baptism, the clothing with a baptismal garment, and the presentation of a lighted candle.

Anointing after Baptism: The only time the anointing with chrism takes place instead of Confirmation is if the person who has been baptized has not yet reached catechetical age. Note that this anointing is on the crown of the head, in contrast to the anointing of Confirmation, which is made on the forehead.

Clothing with a Baptismal Garment: After all the Baptisms have taken place, an assistant may hand the white robes to the godparents. With the neophytes standing together, their godparents might step forward with white robes folded in their arms. Together the godparents hand the robes to the neophytes while the celebrant says the accompanying prayer, which notes that the neophytes "have been clothed in Christ."

Presentation of a Lighted Candle: Immediately after this, the godparents are given a candle. The celebrant calls the godparents forward to light a candle from the Paschal candle. An assistant may need to take the Paschal candle out of the candle stand to allow the flame to be reached. As with the white garment, the godparents go to the neophytes and hand them the lighted candles as the celebrant prays the accompanying prayer.

Depending on the amount of time needed, the newly baptized may be dismissed to dry off at this time. If this would not provide enough time, they may remain in the sanctuary. If they have been baptized by immersion, they may need towels or robes so they do not get cold.

---

35. RCIA, 227.

Renewal of Baptismal Promises

Invitation: The priest then invites the rest of the assembly to renew their baptismal promises; the candidates for reception into full communion join the assembly. Before the renunciation of sin is made, the candles used at the beginning of the Vigil are relighted from the Paschal candle.

Renunciation of Sin and Profession of Faith: The priest uses the same formulary of renunciation and profession that was used for the elect.

Sprinkling with Baptismal Water: The celebrant sprinkles the faithful with the newly blessed baptismal water while an antiphon or another hymn is sung.

The sprinkling should be done with deliberate and full gestures, making sure that everyone in the assembly is sprinkled. In many parishes, the entire assembly is invited to the baptismal font to renew their Baptism, in place of the sprinkling, although this is not mentioned in the rite.

If the newly baptized have left the assembly, they return at this time, wearing their baptismal garments and carrying their lighted baptismal candles. Their return may be accompanied by a joyful song or antiphon sung by the assembly.

Celebration of Reception

Invitation and Profession by the Candidates: The celebrant invites the candidates for reception and their sponsors to stand before the community and profess the Catholic faith by repeating or saying by memory, "I believe and profess all that the holy Catholic Church believes, teaches, and proclaims to be revealed by God."[36]

Act of Reception: The celebrant addresses each of the candidates by name, "N., the Lord receives you into the Catholic Church. His loving kindness has led you here, so that in the unity of the Holy Spirit / you may have full communion with us in the faith that you have professed in the presence of his family."[37] An appropriate song or antiphon may be sung.

---

36. RCIA, 585.
37. RCIA, 586.

The priest or bishop who baptizes also confers Confirmation.

Celebration of Confirmation

Invitation: The priest or bishop who has conferred Baptism is also to confer Confirmation.

The priest speaks to the newly baptized with their godparents and the newly received with their sponsors, explaining the meaning of Confirmation. He then invites the rest of the assembly to pray for the Spirit who will "anoint them to be more like Christ, the Son of God."[38] A silence of sufficient length to allow for such prayer should follow.

Laying on of Hands and Anointing with Chrism: The priest then extends his hands over all the those to be confirmed and prays the prayer asking the Father to send the fullness of the Spirit upon them. Then, after being brought the chrism, he anoints each on the forehead with the chrism, saying, "N. , be sealed with the gift of the Holy Spirit." While this is being done, the godparents and sponsors place a hand on the confirmands' right shoulder. If several people are being confirmed, the assembly may support the ritual by singing an appropriate antiphon or hymn.

The Liturgy of the Eucharist

The rite notes a number of things about the celebration of the Eucharist on this night. Even though the Litany of the Saints was prayed, the Universal

---

38. RCIA, 589.

Prayer is prayed so the newly baptized may take part, exercising their baptismal priesthood for the first time.[39] On this night, it is most appropriate that the newly baptized bring forth the gifts. On this night they pray the Lord's Prayer with the entire community, "giving expression to the spirit of adoption as God's children that they have received in baptism."[40]

There are special interpolations given in *The Roman Missal* at Ritual Masses, Christian Initiation: Baptism, for Eucharistic Prayers I, II, and III. These interpolations reference the newly baptized and their godparents.[41] Before the Lamb of God, the celebrant may speak briefly to the newly baptized and confirmed, reminding them of the preeminence of the Eucharist in their lives now that they are initiated. Finally, the rite

It is appropriate for the newly baptized and received to be first in the Communion procession.

notes that it is most fitting for the newly baptized, confirmed, and received to come forward in the Communion procession first, to receive the Bread of Life and the Cup of Salvation, that is, Communion under both kinds.[42]

---

39. RCIA, 592.
40. RCIA, 217.
41. RCIA, 242.
42. RCIA, 243.

Reception of Baptized Orthodox Christians

*These churches, although separated from us, yet possess true sacraments,
above all—by apostolic succession—the priesthood and the Eucharist,
whereby they are still joined to us in closest intimacy.*

—*Unitatis redintegratio*, 15

The *Rite of Christian Initiation of Adults* says very little about ministering to Orthodox Christians seeking to be part of the Catholic Church, a more and more common experience in many parishes.

Orthodox Christians should not be confused with members of an Eastern Catholic Church who are already part of the communion of the Catholic Church. There are twenty-four Catholic Churches in the Catholic communion, of which the largest is the Latin Church. These include the Maronite Church, the Melkite Greek Church, and the Greek Byzantine Church, to name a few. All of these Churches are in communion with the pope, and each Church recognizes the sacraments of the others as valid.

Regarding a baptized member of an Orthodox Church, RCIA, 474, states:

> In the case of Eastern [Orthodox]Christians who enter into the fullness of Catholic communion, no liturgical rite is required, but simply a profession of Catholic faith, even if such persons are permitted, in virtue of recourse to the Apostolic See, to transfer to the Latin Rite.

No liturgical rite is required because for the vast majority of Orthodox Christians, Baptism, Confirmation (called "chrismation"), and reception of the Eucharist take place in infancy, all at the same time. Infants in the Orthodox Churches are fully initiated, unlike in the Roman Catholic Church, where infants are baptized and Confirmation and Eucharist are deferred to a later age.

The Catholic Church recognizes the validity of all seven sacraments in the Orthodox Church, and vice versa. No other Confirmation is considered valid by the Catholic Communion except for the Orthodox.

So, when an Orthodox Christian is incorporated into the Catholic communion, there is no sacramental celebration. They are not confirmed because they have already been validly confirmed; there is no first reception of the Eucharist because they have already received the Eucharist in infancy. So by what action are they incorporated into Catholicism? As paragraph 474, states, they "simply" profess the Catholic faith; that is, they publicly recite the Nicene Creed and the additional profession of faith, "I believe and profess all that the holy Catholic Church believes, teaches, and proclaims to be revealed by God."[1] No other liturgical rite is necessary.

What can be tricky is identifying where in the Catholic Communion the person(s) now belongs. *Code of Canons of the Eastern Churches*[2] specifically addresses this in canon 35: "Baptized non-Catholics [i.e., Orthodox Christians] coming into full communion with the Catholic Church should retain and practice their own rite everywhere in the world and should observe it as much as humanly possible." This means that Orthodox Christians who wish to be incorporated into the Catholic Communion, do not actually come into the Latin Church. They transfer to the corresponding Eastern Catholic Church, which is part of the Catholic Communion. This action allows that person to participate in the sacramental and liturgical life of the Roman Catholic parish of which they seek to be a part.

For example, should a member of the Greek Orthodox Church wish to be part of the Catholic Communion, he or she would not be incorporated into the Latin Church. Instead, he or she would be ascribed to the Greek Catholic Church. The Greek Catholic Church is Eastern Rite Catholic, part of the Catholic Communion. The same would hold for a Russian Orthodox person. He or she would be ascribed to the Russian Greek Catholic Church.

The term "be ascribed to" is very important, as that is the language that would be used in the parish's baptismal register in recording the person's transfer to the Catholic Communion. Furthermore, the notation in the register would include the corresponding Eastern Catholic Church to which the person is being ascribed. This terminology is very important, and care needs to be taken in the recording in the parish's baptismal register.

Obviously, the process of ministering to Eastern Rite Christians is an intricate process. Before anything else, contact the chancery of the diocese for consultation and direction.

---

1. RCIA, 491.
2. *Code of Canons of the Eastern Churches,* Canon Law Society of America, 2001.

Frequently Asked Questions

Becoming Catholic

1. How is the whole parish involved in Christian initiation?

Parishioners take part in the Christian initiation process through their prayer, presence, and participation. Those seeking to become members of the Church appreciate the joyful welcome that parishioners offer them through warm words extended at parish and community events. Members of the parish should be encouraged to keep the catechumens in their prayer and to greet them whenever the opportunity presents itself.

Parishioners also may lend assistance to the initiation team in a variety of ways. Initiation leaders are always seeking catechists and sponsors, people willing to help with prayer or set up the space for catechesis, and volunteers to assist with hospitality at the various rites and at the catechetical sessions.

Members of parish organizations also could reach out to the catechumens, introducing them to others involved in the community's activities. Parish councils, the school board, choirs, and book, prayer, and parents' groups, and other organizations could invite the catechumens individually or as a group to meet the members (and not be pressured into joining) and socialize. Conversely, members of those groups could be invited to participate in a catechetical session and talk about how their ministry is an expression of faith. Catechumens should always be invited to parish social events.

2. How are people attracted to the Catholic Church?

People are attracted to the Church through hearing the message of Jesus Christ and seeing it lived out. Sometimes they hear the word first, but often they see it lived out first. Many are attracted by the Church's social ministry at an international, national, or local level. Many are attracted by the kindness and integrity of an individual Catholic, or by their hope in difficult times. Others are attracted by the beauty and reverence of our liturgies, or even the beauty of our churches. Some hear the wise words of a pope or bishop in the media. Some pick up a Bible or a book by a theologian or spiritual writer and want to know more. Some fall in love with a Catholic and want to establish a home unified in faith.

However a person comes to a parish, it is always the work of the Holy Spirit, which we are called to support and respond to.

3. What if the Church does not recognize as valid the Baptism of someone seeking to become Catholic?

A person may be attracted to Catholicism because of the kindness members of the Church have shown.

If the Catholic Church does not recognize the validity of the Baptism of the person who has come seeking membership, that person is treated canonically as a catechumen. Care must be taken to explain the situation to the person and to deal with it pastorally. If the person is well catechized in the Christian faith, an abbreviated catechumenate may be appropriate. If a festive celebration of Baptism would be a source of discord to the person or their family, a simpler celebration might be considered.

4. How does a person prove they were baptized?

The usual way to prove that one is baptized is by the presentation of a certificate or letter from the community at which the Baptism took place. In the absence of such proof, the testimony of a parent or other person who was present at the event may suffice, or even the testimony of the person, if the individual was old enough to remember and can recall the event sufficiently. Other evidence such as photos or a record in a family Bible or an inscription in a gift or card given at the time may serve. As a last resort, the person may need to be baptized conditionally in a private setting.

Children

1. How are children of catechetical age initiated into the Church?

Children of catechetical age are considered, for purposes of Christian initiation, to be adults.[1] Their formation should follow the general pattern of the

catechumenate as far as possible. Given their young age, a catechumenate for children may need to be longer than one designed for mature adults.[2]

The permission of the parents, or at least one of them, is required before they are accepted into the catechumenate and before they are initiated into the Church. Parents are encouraged to participate in the process of formation to whatever extent they are able and to offer the support and example the children will need.[3]

2. How are baptized Christian children of catechetical age received into the full communion of the Catholic Church?

Children of catechetical age are initiated into the Church through a catechumenal process adapted for their age and development.

Because children of catechetical age are considered, for purposes of Christian initiation to be adults,[4] the Rite of Reception of Baptized Christians into the Full Communion of the Catholic Church[5] is used. Their formation may be similar to unbaptized children preparing for the initiation sacraments. "Some elements of the ordinary catechetical instruction of baptized children before their reception of the sacraments of confirmation and eucharist may be appropriately shared with catechumens of catechetical age."[6]

---

1. CIC, c. 852 §1 and NS, 18.
2. RCIA, 253.
3. RCIA, 254.
4. CIC, c. 852 §1.
5. RCIA, 473–504.
6. NS, 19.

Children of parents being received into the full communion of the Catholic Church are ordinarily received into the Church with their parents. Like the adults, baptized children of catechetical age who are received are to be confirmed at the same liturgy by the priest who received them.

3. How are children below the age of reason received into the full communion of the Catholic Church?

Presuming the children are being received into the Church at the time one or both parents are being received into the Church, nothing is required of them. Their original Baptism, however, is to be recorded into the baptismal register with a note of their becoming Catholic through their parents' initiation into the Church. It is presumed that they would be confirmed and would receive Eucharist along with the other children of the parish at the customary times.

4. Are children who are completing their initiation through Confirmation and Eucharist expected to celebrate the Sacrament of Reconciliation?

Children who were baptized as Roman Catholics are expected to celebrate the Sacrament of Reconciliation before their first reception of the Eucharist.[7] Children who were baptized, but not as Roman Catholics, and are now preparing for reception into the full communion of the Catholic Church should be adequately prepared and encouraged to celebrate the Sacrament of Reconciliation some time before their formal reception into the Roman Catholic Church.[8]

Children who are catechumens preparing for Baptism obviously do not celebrate the Sacrament of Reconciliation prior to Baptism. Nevertheless they should be invited to participate in non-sacramental penitential rites as outlined in RCIA, 291–303, so that they may come to understand the reality of sin and appreciate the comforting message of God's mercy and pardon. Baptized children can be invited to celebrate these penitential rites with children who are catechumens.

---

7. CIC, c. 914 and NS, 27.
8. RCIA, 482, and NS, 36.

Confirmation

1. Who is to be confirmed when baptized or received into the Church?

Adults and children who have reached catechetical age are to be confirmed at the same liturgy at which they are baptized.[9] The Confirmation of a child of catechetical age is not to be delayed so that the child can be confirmed with his or her class. When the time comes, such children can certainly participate in the catechesis for Confirmation with their classmates. In some dioceses, the bishops recognize and bless these children at the parish celebration of Confirmation.

When baptized candidates are received into the full communion of the Roman Catholic Church, they are to be confirmed at the time of their profession of faith and reception. Their Confirmation is not to be deferred.

2. Who has the responsibility to confirm?

The diocesan bishop is the proper minister of the sacraments of initiation for adults. However, any priest who baptizes an individual of catechetical age or older or receives an individual into the full communion of the Catholic Church, by law has the responsibility to confirm this person.[10]

Priests who do not exercise a pastoral office but participate in a catechumenate require a mandate from the diocesan bishop if they are to baptize; they do not require any additional mandate or authorization in order to confirm but have the faculty to confirm from the law, as do priests who baptize in the exercise of the pastoral office.[11]

3. Can a priest confirm a baptized Catholic?

A priest who wishes to confirm a baptized Catholic must explicitly request this faculty from the diocesan bishop.[12] The only exception is in the case of a baptized Catholic who, through no fault of his or her own, has been instructed in a non-Catholic religion or in the case of the re-admission to communion of a baptized Catholic who has been an apostate from the faith.[13]

---

9. RCIA, 215; CIC, cc. 883 2°, 885 §2; NS, 18–19.
10. CIC, cc. 883 2°, 885 §2.
11. NS, 12.
12. CIC, c. 884 §1.
13. CIC, c. 884 §1.

4. **If candidates who are received into full communion have already been confirmed, should they still be confirmed?**

The Roman Catholic Church accepts the Confirmation of only the Orthodox Church and the Old Catholic Church. All others need to be confirmed in the Roman Catholic Church. If there is doubt, pastoral ministers should consult with their chancery.

5. **Is it permissible at one celebration for one priest to baptize and another to confirm?**

No. The faculty to confirm is only granted to the one who baptizes. If there are a large number to be confirmed, the presiding minister may invite other priests to assist him in the anointing according to the norms prescribed in RCIA, 14.

Marriage Concerns

1. **What is required when a catechumen marries a non-Catholic?**

Although no canonical papers are required by Church law and no dispensation needs to be granted, it is strongly encouraged that the prenuptial questionnaire be completed and carefully filed with other parish marriage records. The status of one or both parties as catechumens at the time of the marriage should be noted on the questionnaire. Pastoral ministers should consult with their chancery about any particular diocesan legislation on this matter. Certainly the same pastoral care should be provided for catechumens as for anyone preparing for marriage.

The marriage should be celebrated at a Liturgy of the Word. Chapter 3 of the *Order of Celebrating Matrimony*, "The Order of Celebrating Marriage between a Catholic and a Catechumen or a Non-Christian" is to be used.[14] As the *National Statutes for the Catechumenate* states, the nuptial blessing may be from chapter 1 of the rite, but all references to Eucharistic sharing are to be omitted.[15]

---

14. NS, 10.
15. NS, 10.

The marriage should be properly recorded in the parish marriage record book and in the book of catechumens.

2. When a catechumen marries a Catholic, what is required?

Along with the usual pastoral care offered to all who are preparing for marriage, the Catholic party who marries a catechumen must request a dispensation because of disparity of cult.

3. If a candidate or a catechumen is in an irregular marriage that needs to be convalidated, when should this be done?

The convalidation of any irregular marriage should be completed before the sacraments of initiation are celebrated. One cannot enter into the full sacramental life of the Church unless one is completely free to receive the sacraments. It is pastorally advisable to convalidate the marriage as early in the process as possible.

4. Should divorced and remarried inquirers be accepted into the catechumenate?

Inquirers who are divorced and remarried (or are married to someone who is divorced and remarried) are, in general, free to enter into the catechumenate. The Congregation for the Doctrine of the Faith responded in the affirmative regarding this question on July 11, 1983,[16] while acknowledging that it is a sensitive issue. In such a case, the potential catechumen must understand that he or she (or his or her spouse) will need an annulment before the catechumen can receive the sacraments of initiation, and that the granting of an annulment cannot be guaranteed in time for the next Easter or, possibly, ever.[17] This has the potential to create a great deal of distress. For this reason, some dioceses have issued guidelines directing that people not be accepted into the Order of Catechumens until the needed annulments are

---

16. Cited in "Christian Initiation and Marriage: Some Practical Issues," Patrick R. Lagges. *Catechumenate: A Journal of Christian Initiation,* vol. 15, no. 3 (May 1993), 8.

17. Diocesan tribunals are aware of the desire to have such matters completed in time for the Easter Vigil and work toward that end. But they cannot guarantee the outcome of any particular marriage case nor can they proceed until all the necessary paperwork has been completed.

granted. This does not mean that such a person cannot participate in catechesis and other formation.

However, such individuals cannot be accepted for the Rite of Election unless the annulment is granted. At that rite, the celebrant declares them "to be members of the elect, to be initiated into the sacred mysteries at the next Easter Vigil."[18] Because someone in an irregular marriage cannot be initiated until the marriage has been convalidated, they cannot be elected for the sacraments of initiation at the coming Easter Vigil. The individuals should certainly be encouraged of the probability of a future time.

Pastoral ministers should discuss the marital status of those who come seeking the sacraments of initiation (and their spouses) in personal interviews early in the process. This includes those seeking Baptism, the baptized who seek Confirmation and Eucharist, and those seeking reception into the full communion of the Catholic Church. Such conversations should be handled with pastoral sensitivity to the situation of the individual and respect for the Church's teaching about marriage.

5. Does a divorced catechumen who has not remarried need an annulment?

A catechumen who is neither currently invalidly remarried nor intends to remarry is not in need of a declaration of nullity to be accepted for the Rite of Election. The catechumen should understand that an annulment will be necessary should he or she wish to marry in the future.

6. If a catechumen is engaged to be married, should the initiation process be abbreviated to allow for initiation before marriage is celebrated?

No, in fact, in some cases it may be more appropriate to concentrate on the preparation for Christian marriage and postpone or extend the catechumenate. Christian marriage is a serious vocation and its preparation should not be neglected or weakened because of one's participation in the catechumenate. Catechumens should be aware that they have the right to marry in the Catholic Church even before they are initiated.

---

18. RCIA, 133.

Record Keeping

1. Where are the names of catechumens recorded after the Rite of Acceptance into the Order of Catechumens is celebrated?

Because the catechumens are joined to the Church and are part of the household of Christ,[19] their status is taken seriously. Their names should be recorded in the parish register of catechumens, "along with the names of the sponsors and the minister and the date and place of the celebration."[20]

2. Where are the names of the elect recorded after the sacraments of initiation are celebrated?

Their names are recorded in the parish baptismal register. Notations are recorded in the Confirmation register and also in the Communion register.

3. Where are the names of the baptized Christians who enter into the full communion of the Roman Catholic Church recorded?

The name of the person received into full communion with the Catholic Church by means of a profession of faith is to be recorded in the parish register under the date of profession together with the date and place of the Baptism of the party, along with the other information required for the baptismal register. If the parish maintains a profession of faith register, the name of the person is also recorded in it.

Information is also recorded in the Confirmation and Communion registers.

---

19. RCIA, 47.
20. RCIA, 46.

Other Questions

1. **Are baptized but uncatechized candidates for reception into the full communion of the Roman Catholic Church obligated to celebrate the Sacrament of Penance prior to their profession of faith?**

"If the profession of faith and reception into the full communion take place within Mass, the candidate, according to his or her own conscience, should make a confession of sins beforehand."[21]

Candidates should receive a thorough catechesis on the Sacrament of Reconciliation and be encouraged in their frequent celebration of the sacrament.[22]

2. **Who is the proper minister of the Rite of Election?**

The diocesan bishop is the proper minister of the Rite of Election. If for pastoral reasons the parish priest is to preside at a celebration of the Rite of Election, he is to obtain specific delegation from the diocesan bishop or the appropriate diocesan authority.[23]

3. **Is it possible to dispense from one or two of the Scrutinites?**

For serious pastoral reasons, the diocesan bishop may dispense from one or even two of the Scrutinies. The parish priest should request the dispensation from the diocesan bishop or the appropriate diocesan authority.[24]

---

21. RCIA, 482.
22. NS, 27, and 36.
23. RCIA, 12, and 34.
24. RCIA, 34 §3.

Periods and Steps in the Rite of Christian Initiation of Adults

	First Period	First Step	Second Period
	Period of Evangelization and Precatechumenate	Rite of Acceptance into the Order of Catechumens	Period of the Catechumenate
Time	Indefinite length	When inquirer and community discern readiness	year (including Period of Purification and Enlightenment)
Name	**Inquirer**		**Catechumen**
What occurs during this period or step	Proclamation of the Gospel and Jesus Christ, leading to faith and initial conversion; introduction to the Christian community	Inquirers publicly declare their intention to become members of the Church; Church accepts them as catechumens.	Formation through catechesis, experience of the Christian way of life through familiarity with community, participation in the liturgical life of the community, and participation in the apostolic life of the Church
Rites belonging to the period	No formal rites; individual prayers and blessings may take place as appropriate.		Celebrations of the Word, Blessings, Anointings, Minor Exorcisms

Second Step	Third Period	Third Step	Fourth Period
Rite of Election	Period of Purification and Enlightenment	Celebration of Sacraments of Initiation	Period of Mystagogy
First Sunday of Lent	Lent	Easter Vigil	Easter Time; extended Mystagogy for one year
	Elect		**Neophyte**
In the name of the Church, the bishop judges readiness of catechumens for initiation and declares that they are chosen for sacraments at the next Easter Vigil.	Retreat-like preparation for the celebration of sacraments of initiation	Initiation into the Church through Baptism, Confirmation, and Eucharist	Deepening of understanding of Paschal Mystery though meditation on the Gospel, participation in the Eucharist, and doing works of charity.
	Scrutinies, Presentations of the Creed and Lord's Prayer, Preparatory Rites on Holy Saturday		Sunday Masses of Easter Time; celebrations near Pentecost and anniversary of initiation; Mass with the bishop

RESOURCES

Church Documents and Ritual Books

- *Ad gentes*, the Decree on the Missionary Activity of the Church, one of the documents proceeding from the Second Vatican Council, was promulgated by Pope Paul VI on December 7, 1965. It describes the mission to spread the Gospel to the whole world as the very essence of the Church's nature. It also describes the catechumenate as "a period of formation in the entire christian life" (14).

- *Evangelii nuntiandi* is an Apostolic Exhortation of Pope Paul VI. It followed upon the 1974 Third General Assembly of the Synod of Bishops, which focused on evangelization. This document, which emphasized the work of evangelization as belonging to the whole Church, was promulgated December 8, 1975, ten year and a day after *Ad gentes*.

- *Lumen gentium*, the Dogmatic Constitution on the Church, was one of the four constitutions of the Second Vatican Council, promulgated by Pope Paul VI on November 21, 1964. It describes the structure and nature of the Church.

- *Catechism of the Catholic Church*, Second Edition. Washington, DC: United States Conference of Catholic Bishops, 1997. Summary of Catholic Church teaching, including a major section on the sacraments.

- *Code of Canon Law: Latin-English Edition: Second Edition.* Washington, DC: United States Conference of Catholic Bishops, 1997. The comprehensive volume includes the major Church laws and legal principles directing the mission of the Catholic Church (Latin or Roman Rite). The *Code* guides how the Church functions, and governs the celebration of the sacraments, the role of the People of God, and the structures that are important to the Church's life.

- *Code of Canons of the Eastern Churches: Latin-English Edition.* Canon Law Society of America, 2001. This book provides the universal law for the Eastern Catholic Churches, which was promulgated in 1990.

- *Rite of Christian Initiation of Adults.* Edition for use in the dioceses of the United States of America. Chicago: Liturgy Training Publications, 1988. This is the official ritual for initiating adults and children of catechetical age, for preparing uncatechized, baptized adults for the sacraments of Confirmation and the reception of the Eucharist for the first time, and for receiving baptized people into the full communion of the Catholic Church. It contains all the directives and guidelines for these situations. Every priest, deacon, and initiation director should have a copy.

- *Rito de iniciación cristiana de adultos.* Spanish edition of the *Rite of Christian Initiation of Adults* for use in the dioceses of the United States of America, 1991. Ritual and study editions are published by the United States Conference of Catholic Bishops.

- *Sacrosanctum concilium,* the *Constitution on the Sacred Liturgy,* was promulgated by Pope Paul VI on December 4, 1963, the first document to proceed from the Second Vatican Council. It called for the renewal of the liturgical life of the Catholic Church, including the reestablishment of the catechumenate.

Pastoral Resources

- Augustine of Hippo. *Instructing Beginners in Faith,* translated by Raymond Caning, Augustine Heritage Institute, 2007. *Instructing Beginners in Faith* was St. Augustine's response to a deacon who wanted help communicating the faith to inquirers. The reflections that St. Augustine used to relay the heart of Christian faith have been adapted throughout the centuries for many contexts. These writings continue to be relevant today.

- Birmingham, Mary. *Year-Round Catechumenate.* Chicago: Liturgy Training Publications, 2003. Mary Birmingham encourages readers to rethink the common model of a Christian initiation program based on the school year. Since the process of initiation exists at the heart of the Church's life, she argues that it should be on the same schedule as the Church. Guiding readers step-by-step through the periods and rites of the initiation process, Birmingham offers pastors, initiation teams, and liturgy committees all the resources needed to imagine, understand, and implement a year-round catechumenate.

- Clay, Michael. *A Harvest for God: Christian Initiation in the Rural and Small-Town Parish.* Chicago: Liturgy Training Publications, 2003. Christian initiation teams in rural areas and small towns will find in this book an approach that is appropriate to the situation and culture of the parish. Any parish with a limited number of people and resources will find *A Harvest for God* useful.

- Galipeau, Jerry. *Apprenticed to Christ: Activities for Practicing the Catholic Way of Life.* Franklin Park, IL: World Library Publications, 2007. This book offers suggested ways those in the process of initiation can be integrated into the life of the parish, making use of the various ministries, outreaches, and activities already established in the parish. This collection of activities is rooted in paragraph 75 of the RCIA, and is geared toward the Sundays of the liturgical year.

- Galipeau, Jerry, editor. *The Impact of the RCIA: Stories, Reflections, Challenges.* Chicago: World Library Publications, 2008. A wealth of articles provide firsthand accounts on Christian initiation from many aspects—global, liturgical, catechetical, musical, Hispanic, African American, rural, urban, episcopal, and ecumenical.

- Huck, Gabe. *The Three Days: Parish Prayer in the Paschal Triduum,* Revised. Chicago: Liturgy Training Publications, 1992. This is a thorough exploration of all the moments that make up the great Paschal Triduum. It gives a solid theology and spirituality of the whole three-day feast, as it can be lived out in a parish setting. This approach provides a solid context for the parish's initiation ministry to see and understand its place in the observance of these most holy days.

- Huels, John. *The Catechumenate and the Law: A Pastoral and Canonical Commentary for the Church in the United States.* Chicago: Liturgy Training Publications, 1994. As a rite of the Church, the RCIA is a canonical document as well as a liturgical one. This eminent canonist examines how the law affects persons (candidates, catechumens, ministers, children, sponsors, and godparents) and situations (invalid or doubtful Baptism and Confirmations, marriage cases, delaying Confirmation, and record keeping), offering pastoral and canonical guidance.

- Hughes, Kathleen. *Saying Amen: A Mystagogy of Sacrament.* Chicago: Liturgy Training Publications, 1994. The author shows how our experience of the sacraments opens the doors to God's transformative power, through Christ and in the Spirit. This book gives a wonderfully accessible approach to seeing how, as Catholics, we really are called to live and live out of a sacramental life.

- Joncas, Jan Michael. *Forum Essays*. No. 4, *Preaching the Rites of Christian Initiation*. Chicago: Liturgy Training Publications, 1994. In the four chapters in this volume, Joncas defines liturgical preaching, outlines the forms liturgical preaching may take in the rites of Christian initiation, gives a process for preparing liturgical preaching, and provides models of such preaching.

- Kavanagh, Aidan. *The Shape of Baptism: The Rite of Christian Initiation*. Collegeville, MN: Pueblo Publishing Company, Inc., 1978. While Kavanagh offers an analysis of Roman initiatory tradition in this book, the commentary also is a pastoral one.

- Lewinski, Ron. *Welcoming the New Catholic*. Chicago: Liturgy Training Publications, 1993. This is a thorough, basic introduction to the cate-chumenal process. It begins with stating a pastoral approach to ministering to those desiring to become members of the Church that describes the steps and stages outlined in the RCIA with that approach in mind.

- Madigan, Shawn. *Forum Essays*. No. 5, *Liturgical Spirituality and the Rite of Christian Initiation of Adults*. Chicago: Liturgy Training Publications, 1997. The five chapters in this volume consider the rites of Christian initiation as formative and expressive of a liturgical spirituality.

- McMahon, J. Michael. *The Rite of Christian Initiation of Adults: A Pastoral Liturgical Commentary*. Revised edition. Washington, D.C.: Federation of Diocesan Liturgical Commissions, 2002. This study guide presents documentation from the *Rite of Christian Initiation of Adults* and other pertinent Church documents, commentary, and study questions for every aspect of the initiation of adults,

- Mitchell, Nathan D. *Forum Essays*. No. 2, *Eucharist as Sacrament of Initiation*. Chicago: Liturgy Training Publications, 1994. Within three chapters, Nathan Mitchell considers the meaning of the neophyte's participation in the paschal meal.

- Morris, Thomas H. *The RCIA: Transforming the Church; A Resource for Pastoral Implementation*. Revised and updated edition. New York: Paulist Press, 1997. If every RCIA minister is to have the *Rite of Christian Initiation of Adults* in one hand, then having Morris' book in the other hand will round it all out. This book is an excellent resource that takes the vision of the RCIA and shows *how* that vision can take shape in the parish setting.

- Oakham, Ron A., editor. *One at the Table: The Reception of Baptized Christians*. Chicago: Liturgy Training Publications, 1995. This book begins with five articles offering theological foundations for understanding the issues surrounding the reception of the baptized. Oakham then presents a pastoral plan for ministering to the baptized person seeking reception into the full communion of the Catholic Church.

- Paprocki, Joe and D. Todd Williamson. *Great Is the Mystery: The Formational Power of Liturgy*. Chicago: Liturgy Training Publications, 2012. Catechesis and liturgy are connected in this book that walks readers through the foundational principles of a Catholic liturgical life. The authors, experts in the field, break open the principles, making them accessible and understandable. They also explore the various elements and dynamics of a liturgical spirituality, an understanding of liturgy, the liturgical year, and give an in-depth look at each part of the weekly celebration of the parish Eucharist.

- Senseman, Rita Burns, Victoria M. Tufano, Paul Turner, D. Todd Williamson, *The Rite of Christian Initiation of Adults with Children*. Chicago: Liturgy Training Publications, 2017. The authors consider the adaptions made for children in Part II of the *Rite of Christian Initiation of Adults* as well as the appropriateness of including children with adults in the rites. Also provides guidance for receiving children into the full communion of the Catholic Church.

- Turner, Paul. *The Hallelujah Highway: A History of the Catechumenate*. Chicago: Liturgy Training Publications, 2000. Turner's rich narrative recounts the history of the catechumenate through stories of the people and documents that shaped the rites of initiation from the earliest days of the Church to the present.

- Vincie, Catherine. *Forum Essays*, No. 1, *The Role of the Assembly in Christian Initiation*. Chicago: Liturgy Training Publications, 1993. This volume considers the responsibility of the assembly as it is laid out in the order of initiation.

- Wagner, Nick. *The Way of Faith: A Field Guide for the RCIA Process*. Twenty-Third Publications, 2008. Readers will find a solid overview of the process of initiation as it can be implemented in the parish setting. Wagner does an excellent job of addressing each of the periods of the initiation process and addressing the who, what, where, when, why, and how of each period.

- Tufano, Victoria M., ed. *Celebrating the Rites of Adult Initiation: Pastoral Reflections.* Chicago: Liturgy Training Publications, 1992. This collection of essays offers the insights of Kathleen Hughes, Michael Joncas, Rita Ferrone, James Moudry, Catherine Mowry Lacugna, Mark Francis, Marguerite Main, Ronald Oakham, and Edward Foley on the rites of initiation. These essays look at the Scrutinies, the Rite of Acceptance, and the Presentations. Also included are commentaries on the Minor Exorcisms, the taking of a new name, and the Liturgy of the Word.

Theological Resources

- Ferrone, Rita. *Forum Essays.* No. 2, *On the Rite of Election*, Chicago: Liturgy Training Publications, 1994. In this series of essays, the author explores the theology of the Rite of Election and its place in the initiation process.

- Johnson, Maxwell E., *Images of Baptism.* CreateSpace Independent Publishing Platform, 2013. In the four essays in this book, the author studies key baptismal images and metaphors in Scripture and liturgical tradition.

- Sieverding, Dale J. *Forum Essays*, No. 7, *The Reception of Baptized Christians: A History and Evaluation.* Chicago: Liturgy Training Publications, 2011. In examining the history of the reception of baptized Christians, the essays move from the patristic period, medieval liturgical books, modern history, the Second Vatican, to the post-conciliar development of the ritual.

- Turner, Paul. *When Other Christians Become Catholic.* Collegeville, MN: The Liturgical Press, 2007. The author presents historical and ecumenical contexts in which to understand what we do when we receive baptized Christians into the full communion of the Catholic Church. He challenges us to examine our practices to reflect the true nature of what we are doing when we receive other Christians into the Catholic Church and in this way to witness to the unity of Christians as it is now and as it is to be.

- Yarnold, Edward, SJ, *The Awe-Inspiring Rites of Initiation: The Origins of the RCIA*, Second Edition, Collegeville, MN: Liturgical Press, 1994. *The Awe-Inspiring Rites of Initiation* first came out in 1972 but was recast two decades later to correspond with the *Rite of Christian Initiation of Adults*. In this book, students of liturgy and catechists will gain a better understanding of the RCIA as they learn about the catechumenal practices of the fourth century and read the sermons on the sacraments preached by Cyril, Ambrose, Chrysostom, and Theodore. Through these sermons, the Church Fathers guided neophytes to contemplate the Christian mysteries.

GLOSSARY

Adult: For the purpose of sacramental initiation, a person who has reached the age of reason (also called the age of discretion or catechetical age), usually regarded to be seven years of age, is an adult. A person who has reached that age is to be initiated into the Church according to the *Rite of Christian Initiation of Adults* and receive the three sacraments of initiation together, although the catechesis should be adapted to the individual's needs. Before this age, the person is considered an infant and is baptized using the *Rite of Baptism for Children*.

Apostles' Creed: The ancient baptismal statement of the Church's faith. The questions used in the celebration of Baptism correspond to the statements of the Apostles' Creed.

Baptismal Font: The pool or basin at which the Sacrament of Baptism is administered.

Blessing: Any prayer that praises and thanks God. In particular, *blessing* describes those prayers in which God is praised because of some person or object, and thus the individual or object is seen to have become specially dedicated or sanctified because of the prayer of faith.

Book of the Elect: A book into which the names of those catechumens who have been chosen, or elected, for initiation at the next Easter Vigil, are written at or before the Rite of Election.

Book of the Gospels: A ritual book from which the passages from the accounts of the Gospel prescribed for Masses on Sundays, solemnities, feasts of the Lord and of the saints, and ritual Masses are proclaimed; also called an evangeliary.

Candidate: In its broadest definition, the term refers to anyone preparing to receive a sacrament. In the *Rite of Christian Initiation of Adults*, the term is used as a general designation for adults who are expressing an interest in the Catholic faith, whether baptized or not. In common usage, *candidate* is used for a baptized person preparing for reception into the full communion of the Catholic Church; an unbaptized person inquiring about preparing for Christian initiation is called an *inquirer.*

Catechesis: Instruction and spiritual formation in the faith, teachings, and traditions of the Church.

Catechetical age: Usually considered to be about seven years of age; also called the age of reason or the age of discretion. For the purpose of Christian initiation, a person who has reached catechetical age is considered an adult and is to be initiated into the Church according to the *Rite of Christian Initiation of Adults.*

Catechumen: An unbaptized person who has declared his or her intention to prepare for the sacraments of initiation and has been accepted into the Order of Catechumens. Catechumens, though not yet fully initiated, are joined to the Church and are considered part of the household of Christ.

Catechumenate: The second of four periods in the process of Christian initiation as described in the *Rite of Christian Initiation of Adults.* The period begins with the Rite of Acceptance into the Order of Catechumens. It is a period of nurturing and growth of the catechumens' faith and conversion to God in Christ. Sometimes the term *catechumenate* is used to refer to the entire initiation process.

Celebrant: The presiding minister at worship.

Child: For the purposes of Christian initiation, one who has not yet reached the age of discernment (age of reason, presumed to be about seven years of age) and therefore cannot profess personal faith.

Chrism: One of the three Holy Oils. It is consecrated by the bishop at the Chrism Mass and used at the Baptism of infants, at Confirmation, at the ordination of priests and bishops, and at the dedication of churches and altars. Chrism is scented, usually with balsam.

Companion: In the Christian initiation process with children of catechetical age, a baptized child of an age similar to the child catechumen who takes part in the catechetical group and accompanies the catechumen in the rites.

Confirmation: The sacrament that continues the initiation process begun in Baptism and marks the sealing of the Holy Spirit. It is administered through an anointing with chrism on the forehead with the words, "*N.*, be sealed with the Gift of the Holy Spirit," preceded by the imposition of hands.

Dismissal: The final, formal invitation by the deacon or, in his absence, the priest for the assembly to go forth from the liturgical celebration. The word can also refer to the dismissal of the catechumens after the homily at Mass.

Easter Vigil: While the Church keeps watch this night, a fire is lighted, Scriptures are read that tell the story of salvation, the elect receive the Easter sacraments, and all present renew their baptismal promises.

Elect: Catechumens who have been formally called, or elected, by the Church for Baptism, Confirmation, and Eucharist at the next Easter Vigil.

Ephphetha Rite: A rite of opening the ears and the mouth, associated with the celebration of Baptism. The rite, which has its origin in Mark 7:31–37, Jesus' healing of a deaf man, prays that the one being baptized may hear and profess the faith. It may be performed with the elect as part of their preparation on Holy Saturday for initiation at the Easter Vigil or as part of the *Rite of Baptism for Children*.

Exorcism: A prayer or command given to cast out the presence of the devil. The *Rite of Baptism for Children* contains a prayer of exorcism; the *Rite of Christian Initiation of Adults* contains prayers of exorcism as part of the rites belonging to the Period of the Catechumenate and as part of the Scrutinies. There is a *Rite of Exorcism* for use in the case of possession; it may be used only with the express permission of a bishop and only by mandated priest-exorcists.

Evangelization: The continuing mission of the Church to spread the Gospel of Jesus Christ to all people. During the Period of Evangelization and Precatechumenate, evangelization includes invitation, the welcoming, the witness, the sharing of faith, and the proclamation of the Gospel to inquirers.

Faculty: A right granted to enable a person to do something, usually referring to a right granted to a priest or deacon by law or by the bishop.

Godparents: Members of the Christian community, chosen for their good example and their close relationship to the one being baptized, who are present at the celebration of Baptism and provide guidance and assistance to the one baptized afterward.

Holy Saturday: The Saturday within the Sacred Paschal Triduum. It is a day marked by meditation, prayer, and fasting in anticipation of the Resurrection of the Lord. Several Preparation Rites for the elect who will be receiving the sacraments of initiation at the Vigil are proper to this day.

Immersion: A method of Baptism in which the candidate is submerged either entirely or partially in the baptismal water.

Infusion: A method of Baptism in which the baptismal water is poured over the head of the candidate.

Inquirer: An unbaptized adult who is in the very first stage of the process of Christian initiation.

Inquiry: Another name given to the Period of Evangelization and Precatechumenate, the first period or stage in the process of Christian initiation.

Initiation: The process by which a person enters the faith life of the Church—from the catechumenate through the normally continuous celebration of the entrance rites of Baptism, Confirmation, and the Eucharist.

Laying on of hands: A gesture of blessing or invocation recorded in the New Testament in conjunction with prayer (for example, Acts 13:3; 2 Timothy 1:6). The gesture is performed by extending both hands forward with the palms turned downward. Depending on the circumstances, the hands may be placed on the person's head or stretched out over a group of people or over an object.

Litany of the Saints: A litany that calls upon the saints to pray for the Church, believed to be the most ancient litany in the Church's worship.

Minor Rites: Rites during the catechumenate, which include the Rite of Exorcism, Rite of Blessing, and Rite of Anointing.

Mystagogy: The postbaptismal catechesis given to the newly baptized during Easter Time, wherein the neophyte and the local Church share the meaning of the initiatory mysteries and experience.

National Statutes for the Catechumenate: A document issued by the United States Bishops in 1986, and confirmed by the Apostolic See in 1988, constituting particular law for the implementation of the RCIA in the United States.

Neophyte: One who is recently initiated. It comes from the word meaning *new plant* or *twig, a new sprout on a branch.* After the Period of Mystagogy the new Catholic is no longer called neophyte.

Oil of Catechumens: The oil, blessed by the bishop at the Chrism Mass (or for pastoral reasons by the priest before the anointing) to be used in the anointing of the catechumens during the process of initiation.

Order of Catechumens: The canonical group to which an unbaptized adult who is preparing to receive the sacraments of initiation belongs after celebrating the *Rite of Acceptance into the Order of Catechumens.*

Paschal Mystery: The saving mystery of Christ's Passion, Death, and Resurrection. It is the mystery that is celebrated and made present in every liturgy, and the mystery that every Christian is to imitate and be united with in everyday life.

Penance: The sacrament by which the baptized, through the mercy of God, receive pardon for their sins and reconciliation with the Church. This sacrament is most commonly celebrated by the private confession of sin and expression of sorrow by a penitent to a confessor, who then offers absolution. It is also commonly called confession or the Sacrament of Reconciliation.

Postbaptismal catechesis: Mystagogical catechesis, instruction given to the newly baptized, or neophytes, to help them deepen their understanding of the faith primarily through reflection on the sacraments they celebrated at Easter.

Precatechumenate: A period of indeterminate length that precedes acceptance into the Order of Catechumens. In the *Rite of Christian Initiation of Adults,* this time is called the Period of Evangelization and Precatechumenate; it is also referred to as inquiry.

Preparation Rites: Various rites that can be celebrated with the elect on Holy Saturday in proximate preparation for the celebration of the sacraments of initiation at the Easter Vigil that evening.

Presentations: Rites whereby the Church entrusts the Creed and the Lord's Prayer, the ancient texts that express the heart of the Church's faith, to the elect.

Proper: Those texts in the Mass and in the Liturgy of the Hours that are particular to a given day.

Purification and Enlightenment: The period of final preparation for unbaptized adults journeying toward initiation in the Catholic Church. It is a time of intense spiritual preparation marked by the celebration of the Scrutinies and the Presentations. It usually coincides with Lent.

RCIA: *Rite of Christian Initiation of Adults,* the official rite of the Roman Catholic Church for initiation of adults and children of catechetical age and the reception of baptized candidates.

Reception of Baptized Christians into the Full Communion of the Catholic Church: The liturgical rite for receiving into the full communion of the Catholic Church an adult who was validly baptized in a non-Catholic Christian community.

Register of Catechumens: The book in which the names of those unbaptized adults who have been accepted as catechumens is recorded. The names of the sponsors and the minister and the date and place of the celebration of the *Rite of Acceptance into the Order of Catechumens* should also be recorded. Each parish should have a Register of Catechumens.

Renunciation of Sin: The ritual questioning that precedes the Profession of Faith made at Baptism or in the renewal of Baptism. There are two alternate forms of the formula for the renunciation of sin, each of which consists of three questions that center on the rejection of Satan and his works.

Rite of Baptism for Children: The ritual book that gives the rites for the Baptism of children who have not yet attained the age of discretion (the age of reason), presumed to be about age seven.

Rite of Christian Initiation of Adults (RCIA): The ritual book, part of the Roman Ritual, that gives the norms, directives, and ritual celebrations for initiating unbaptized adults and children who have reached catechetical age into Christ and incorporating them into the Church. The RCIA prescribes a sequence of periods and rites by which candidates transition from one stage to another, which culminate in the celebration of the sacraments of initiation, usually at the Easter Vigil.

Rite of Election: The second step for unbaptized adults preparing for the sacraments of initiation, also called the Enrollment of Names. The rite closes the period of the catechumenate and marks the beginning of the Period of Purification and Enlightenment, which usually corresponds to Lent. With this rite the Church makes its election, or choice, of the catechumens to receive the sacraments. The Rite of Election normally takes place on or near the First Sunday of Lent.

Sacraments of Christian initiation: The Sacraments of Baptism, Confirmation, and Eucharist. All three sacraments are necessary to be fully initiated into the Church. Adults, including children of catechetical age, receive the three sacraments in one liturgy when being initiated into the Church.

Sacred Paschal Triduum: The three-day celebration of the Paschal Mystery of Christ that is the high point and center of the entire liturgical year. The Paschal Triduum begins with the Evening Mass of the Lord's Supper on Holy Thursday, solemnly remembers Christ's Death on Good Friday, reaches its zenith at the Easter Vigil with the Baptism of the elect into the mystery of Christ's Death and Resurrection, and concludes with Evening Prayer of Easter Sunday.

Scrutiny: A rite of self-searching and repentance intended to heal whatever is weak or sinful in the hearts of the elect, and to strengthen all that is good, in preparation for their reception of the Easter sacraments. The Scrutinies are exorcisms by which the elect are delivered from the power of Satan and protected against temptation. Usually, three rites of Scrutiny are celebrated.

Sending of the Catechumens for Election: An optional rite that may be celebrated before the catechumens take part in the Rite of Election. The rite, which usually takes place at Mass, expresses the parish community's approval and support of the catechumens' election by the bishop.

Sponsor: In the Christian initiation of adults, one who accompanies a person seeking admission as a catechumen. The sponsor is someone who knows the candidate and is able to witness to the candidate's moral character, faith, and intention. He or she accompanies the candidate at the Rite of Acceptance into the Order of Catechumens and continues to accompany and support the person through the Period of the Catechumenate. In the celebration of the Sacrament of Confirmation with those who were baptized in infancy, the sponsor presents a person being confirmed to the minister of the sacrament. After the celebration of the sacrament, the sponsor helps the individual live in accord with their baptismal promises

White garment: The clothing, often similar to an alb, which is given to someone immediately after Baptism. This garment is a sign that the newly baptized person has put on new life in Christ. It is used in the Baptism of both adults and children.